THE GENTLEMAN CHAMELEON

P. A. Schweizer

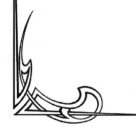

DISCLAIMER

This is a fictional story. Names, characters, places, and events are totally the invention of the author's imagination. Therefore, any similarity to actual occurrences or people living or dead is entirely coincidental.

ACKNOWLEDGMENTS

First and foremost, I am eternally grateful to my wonderful parents whose love and support has made me the strong and motivated person I am today. It was their nurturing that gave me the courage and determination to accomplish my dreams.

However, if it were not for the dedication of my true friend and editor, Kim Cherevas, who believed in me from the moment I showed her my original manuscript, I would not have completed this undertaking. She lived, breathed, and dreamt this book with me, while we both enjoyed watching the characters evolve. For this and more, I will always be thankful to Kim.

I would also like to thank my proofreaders, who took on the painstaking task: my longtime friends, Camille Nebus, Robert Trembley, Helen Babits, Judy Larocca and my sister Ann Dunn, who assisted me while she was ill. I sincerely appreciate all their corrections and poignant suggestions.

I also appreciate the good eyes of the 'Detail Queen' my niece, Theresa Brewer-Dougherty. I extend my personal devotion to the exceptional tag team, Jennifer, and David Mayer who uncovered a profound publishing error.

It is with much love that I thank my multitalented nephew Rory Sevajian Jr. for his designing input which surpassed my expectations. Many thanks to Alexandra Cherevas for her ingenious creation of the chameleon scales for my cover.

Lastly, I would like to thank my mother-in-law, Vera, for being the catalyst of my writing career.

For all the Katies and Julies…

This book is dedicated to my two Alpha and Omegas, who have inspired me to write this book:

J.C., the only man who has never let me down, and to my son, Michael, the CHAMP!

I love you both so very much.

SUNDAY, OCTOBER 2

The two women could have been mistaken for high school girls as they sat giggling on the stoop of Katie's brownstone. Katie and her childhood friend Ann Marie were reminiscing about their earlier carefree years, life BCC— life before commitment and children.

"What were we thinking?" laughed Katie.

"Life couldn't have been any better way back when," quipped Ann Marie. "And to think we gave it all up, and for what?"

At that moment, two darling little girls came running toward them, flailing their arms and pleading, "Mommy, Mommy, the ice cream man is coming! Can we get something?"

Katie was the first to address her daughter, Laura. "Not today. Your father should be home any minute, and we'll be eating dinner then."

Ann Marie was quick to add, "Suzie, we'll be leaving soon. Grandma is waiting for us to get home." Luckily, the girls' attention was quickly diverted by a boy showing off on his bike, and the ice cream was fast forgotten.

Ann Marie lived a couple of blocks away in the house where she grew up. She and Suzie had moved back in with her mother after Ann Marie's divorce. Their home was conveniently next door to Katie's parents, which kept the two friends in constant contact. They were both thirty-two years old and had married older boys from town, Matt, who was now thirty-four, and Rory, who was thirty-five. They had grown up on the same street where Matt and Katie currently lived but further down in a much less affluent section at that time. Ann Marie and Katie had acted as maids of honor at each other's wedding. The women had, even more, to share now. Five years earlier, they had delivered their daughters within a day of each other. They experienced their pregnancies together; later, while Ann Marie suffered through her separation and divorce, Katie had embraced Ann Marie's pain as her own. They had shared so much over the years that they were more like sisters than friends. They vowed never to leave Hoboken.

Suddenly, Laura squealed "Daddy, Daddy!" as her father came bounding down the street toward them. He scooped the little girls up, one in each arm, and planted a big kiss on each of their cheeks.

"I envy you, Katie," said Ann Marie. "You have the most wonderful, handsome, and attentive husband in all of Hudson County. He's always the perfect gentleman." I always admire the way he opens the car door for you and helps you on with your coat. I can't remember Rory ever doing that for me."

"Hush; don't let him hear you say that. I like to keep him humble. Besides, I plan on keeping him for a while—like for the rest of my life!" declared Katie, admiring him as he approached.

Matt was six foot three with dark brown hair and sexy brown puppy eyes that could charm any girl, young or old. He was not only impressive in stature but also extremely polite. He commanded attention whenever he entered a room, yet he appeared unaware of his appeal. Matt and Katie made an enchanting couple since her looks were just as striking, yet contrasting with his. She was a petite and shapely black-haired beauty with sparkling green eyes. They were both people magnets and enjoyed a busy social life with many friends.

"Hello, sunshine," said Katie as Matt gave her a quick kiss on the lips. "How was your day?"

"Working on Sundays is never any fun," he answered. "Something came up today; I'll tell you about it later," he said as he bent over to give Ann Marie a peck on the cheek. "What have you ladies been up to today, besides sitting out here enjoying the scenery and keeping tabs on the neighborhood?"

"Someone has to do it," quipped Ann Marie. "In fact, we take our job very seriously. But now, I think it's time for Suzie and me to go home. I'll be sure to let you know if anything exciting happens on my block. Suzie, say your good-byes so we can go. Talk to you tomorrow, Katie. Be good, Matt," she said as she started walking away.

"Wait a sec, and I'll walk you, two young ladies, home," Matt said as he started towards them.

"I truly appreciate your offer, but we only have to walk a few blocks," answered Ann Marie.

"You're welcome," he said.

They both watched Ann Marie and Suzie as they walked away.

"It's a shame that Ann Marie and Rory didn't work out. I really enjoyed our times with them. Even our vacations together were great. It was a perfect setup; we each had someone to hang out with. You had Ann Marie, I had Rory, and Laura had Suzie. We were like one big happy family," Matt said.

"I guess we'll never know what possessed him to leave her for that younger girl who's dumped him now," said Katie. "It's like that old expression—'the grass looks greener on the other side of the fence, but it still has to be mowed.' To think what he gave up for a fling, not to mention the people he hurt."

"I totally agree that he made a big mistake, but I still can't understand why she wouldn't forgive him and take him back when he came crawling," Matt said. "He still loves her and Suzie."

"Are you kidding?" Katie exclaimed. "I don't blame her at all. Do you think I would ever forgive you if you did that to me?" The Reilly family sat out a minute more before retiring to their own apartment on the second floor.

Once upstairs, Matt slumped into an easy chair. His demeanor changed when he saw the condition of the apartment and found his dinner hadn't been made.

"Katie, please tell me what you do all day besides sitting outside and gossip with your girlfriend? Honey, can't I please come home just once to a clean home and dinner on the table?"

Katie defended herself quickly, "C'mon, that's not fair, Matt! Today was the first nice day in a long time, and we took the girls to the park right after church." Matt dropped the subject because he had something more important to discuss later. Besides, he knew Katie lacked domestic skills before he married her. He remembered how she kept (or didn't keep) her room at her parents' house. Maybe he would surprise her one of these days with a cleaning lady. He thought about it as he slipped into a short snooze while waiting for the pizza to be delivered.

During dinner, Matt decided to break his news. "Girls, I was chosen along with four other guys to be loaned to another utility company in Connecticut for few weeks."

"Why?" gasped Katie.

"Can we go with you, Daddy?" asked Laura.

"No, I'm sorry, sweetie. I'll be sharing a hotel room with another fella. But I will be coming home on weekends. It's only two hours away." He then turned to Katie and explained, "We're going to help restore and repair service up there. Evidently, it's a mess from that nor'easter we had last week. And we thought we had it bad when our lights went out for three hours."

"When are you leaving?"

"Tomorrow."

"Tomorrow!" she exclaimed in shock. "Not much notice, huh? You've already worked seven days straight!"

"I know, and I'm sorry, but duty calls in the morning. They're under tremendous pressure to restore power to the thousands of people without it. Anyway, just think, honey, we can use the extra money to save for our dream house. By the way, they are giving me a generous daily stipend for meals and recreation. I have no clue what they could mean by recreation."

"I just hate when we're apart," whimpered Katie.

"Me too," he agreed, as he leaned over and kissed her.

Matt and Katie had a unique love story that started in high school. Although they were two years apart in age and at school, they ran in the same social circles and shared the same friends. After school each day the kids usually made their way to the waterfront to hang out by the Hudson River. There were empty lots back then where people used to dump their old furniture, car parts, and odds and ends. While the empty lots resembling junk yards fascinated children and scavengers of all ages, the spectacular view of the New York skyline attracted everyone.

One day when the teens ventured out on an old decrepit pier to sit and sneak their smokes, Matt slipped and fell in the river. The friends were so busy laughing that they failed to realize that he couldn't swim at all and was actually drowning. He flailed his arms and panicked, swallowing gulps of water as he shouted for help. It was only after Katie jumped in to save him that they understood the severity of the moment. She quickly put her arm around his head and neck and pulled him to safety. Their friends were stupefied as the two trudged out of the water like wet rats, Katie holding a weakened Matt up, as he leaned on her.

They sat on the rocks away from the group, and Matt panted to catch his breath, as he tried to recover from the ordeal. A few seconds more and he might have drowned if it hadn't been for Katie. He looked at her as if for the first time. He then spoke, "Thank you so much; I thought I was a goner there."

She answered him with a smile, "I guess you never took swimming lessons."

He laughed, "What for? I can count on one hand the times I've been in a swimming pool, never mind in a river!" Katie had some idea from remarks that their friends made that Matt came from a very poor background, but that hadn't kept her from loving him since the first time she had set eyes on him in grade school. His near drowning experience created a special bond between them, and from that moment on the two became inseparable; Katie became his anchor and protector. A few years later they were married and began their happily-ever-after life.

Their wedding day was like a real-life fairy tale. Katie's parents cherished their only child and gave her a wedding most girls could only wish for. Katie loved the story of Cinderella, which her father had read to her many times at bedtime. He called her his Cinderella and insisted that a horse-drawn carriage take them to the church where her Prince Charming waited for her at the altar. Walking her down the aisle, he cried at the thought that his little girl was all grown up, but was much relieved that she had picked a wonderful gentleman as her prince. People always commented to him about Matt's politeness. He loved Matt and knew that he was good to his daughter. He prayed Katie and Matt would someday have a little girl to cherish, in the same ways that he had cherished his Katie.

Matt was happy to tuck Laura into bed that night.

"Daddy, I don't want you to go away," Laura moaned.

"I have to, honey. It's for my job," he said as he cradled her in his arms. "I have to earn money so that I can take care of you and Mommy."

"We don't need money, Daddy; we just need you," she insisted, as she hugged him tighter and kissed his cheek.

"And I need you both, too," he said.

"But then why can't we go with you?" she asked.

"Because *you* have to go to school, silly-willy, and I will come home on the weekends anyway," he tried to convince her.

"Alright, then, you can go, but you have to call me every day," she demanded as a stipulation. He read her favorite book, *Sleeping Beauty*, to her. "When I grow up, I'm going to marry a prince just like Mommy did," Laura said. Matt smiled as he hugged his little girl tightly and promised he would call his princess every day while he was away. Content with his reassurance, Laura fell asleep.

Matt looked around the dimly lit room decorated in her favorite colors of soft pinks and purples. Her windows were adorned with delicate lace curtains and prints of Degas' Ballerinas hung on her walls. Her brass bed with white porcelain knobs was dressed in a satiny ruffled duvet which complimented the curtains.

Matt insisted that Laura have a proper nightlight in her room to protect her from the same night demons that he encountered as a child. Eerily, they followed him into his adulthood. He took a last loving look at his sleeping princess before he left her room, content that he had provided her with a safe haven which he had never known as a child.

Katie was propped up on pillows reading a book when he entered their bedroom. He was relieved to see that she had turned *his* night light already. Matt used the excuse of needing light to see his way to the bathroom. He was never able to share the horrors of his childhood, not even with Katie. His sporadic nightmares alarmed her but he always bounced right back as though nothing had happened.

"I'm going to miss that little girl of ours. She just gave me her permission to go as long as I come home on weekends and call her every day," he chuckled.

Katie held out her hand to him saying, "I haven't given you mine yet," as she pulled him into bed with her. There, he took Katie into his arms and began kissing her neck and caressing her breast. It amazed her how he could make her feel each time as though it were their very first time together. She melted into his heated body and soon she succumbed to his gentle and rhythmic thrusts. As they lay elated but spent, she whispered, "Can I have an encore?" Their lovemaking continued into the night, leaving them both exhausted in the morning.

MONDAY, OCTOBER 3

The ride to Connecticut isn't bad at all when you're not driving, thought Matt as he looked out the car window. He was happy that his buddy Kevin had agreed to drive, allowing him to doze. Leaving the girls that morning had been difficult for him, as he had held them tightly while they cried. He would rather have gone without saying good-bye and spared himself the emotion.

He was also relieved when Kevin offered him a ride so that he could leave his car in the shop to be serviced. His mechanic agreed to drop it by the house when it was finished, to avoid any imposition on Katie. It was bad enough that he had to go away, but he didn't want Katie to have to worry about anything more than their precious daughter.

Kevin was a very quiet, easy-going kind of guy who never had too much to say. As the only boy in a family of five children, he had obviously been taught at a young age that it was better to listen than to talk. Matt was surprised that he was still single at the age of thirty-five. After all, he wasn't a bad looking fellow, standing six feet tall with his blonde hair and blue eyes. Matt didn't understand why he was still alone. What were women looking for?

Matt had heard that Kevin had been engaged to a girl that he adored a few years back. He bought her the biggest and best of everything, an enormous diamond engagement ring, and a BMW as a wedding gift, only to be literally left at the altar. Rumor had it that he was never the same after her rejection. Wow, thought Matt, wouldn't he be perfect with Ann Marie! He would have to run that by Katie before mentioning it to Kev. He never pictured himself as a matchmaker. But the more he thought about it, the more he could see Kevin and Ann Marie together and the four of them socializing just like it was before when Rory was still around.

"It won't be long now," said Kevin, "until we're in Litchfield."

"I'm sorry I wasn't much company for you on the ride up, but I didn't sleep that great last night," said Matt.

"No bother," said Kevin. "I-95 moved smoothly and it's been easy sailing so far. Actually, my grandmother grew up in Litchfield, the town where we're staying. I came up here very often with my grandparents as a child to visit relatives and my grandmother's old friends. They took me to all the different historical sites. There's a lot of Revolutionary War history in Litchfield," he explained.

"I didn't realize that," said Matt.

"Yeah, its inland location kept it safe from British attack and enabled the patriots to house loyalist prisoners. I also remember reading in one of the museums that a large statue of King George III was torn down somewhere in NYC, broken into pieces, and brought up here for the local women and children to make into bullets for the war effort. Hey, did you know that the first law school in the country was Litchfield Law School?"

"No, I didn't know that. Now you've piqued my interest. I hope I get a minute to do some sightseeing," Matt said. He loved to get lost in the nostalgia of history. He had spent many hours of his lonely childhood with his imagination immersed in the annals of history.

"I really hope our hotel isn't a dump. I like to feel at home and comfortable."

"I was told we were staying in a bed-and-breakfast-type place. I didn't dare tell Katie that or there would be no keeping her at home. She loves a quaint setup."

Kevin sighed, "Thank God, you and I will be sharing a room. I can't see me having to bunk with any of the other three fellas. What about you?"

Matt answered, "It doesn't matter to me. I just hate to be alone so I try to fit in wherever I go."

"That's true," Kevin agreed, "You are a natural shoo-in with people! I've noticed that about you."

"I learned at an early age," explained Matt. "It was lonely growing up in my house. My mom was always working, so I tried to be home as little as possible. If you ask my childhood friends they would all claim me as an honorary family member. I had so many adopted families over the years that I lost count. I guess that's why I am so adaptable."

"I'd hate to be you at Christmas, having to buy all those gifts!" laughed Kevin.

Matt replied to Kevin's joke by saying, "Funny thing you should say that because I've lost touch with all of them over the years, even though most of us still live in the same town. We all seem to have moved on with our lives." Kevin thought it was very strange that Matt could detach himself so easily from those that were supposedly so kind to him.

"Hey, look, Matt, it's our place. Wow! Looks good, huh?"

"I'll say," agreed Matt. The bed-and-breakfast was ginormous from the outside. It was also a typical New England structure: white clapboard with green shutters and flower boxes outside each window. It had a big wraparound porch boasting sturdy white wicker furniture with puffy comfortable cushions that matched the large awnings over the porch. Despite the magnitude of the storm, the property was well groomed with fall flowers blooming everywhere.

"Looks like they cleaned up the ground nicely compared to some of the places we just passed. I wonder what they do for fun around here?" uttered Matt. "Not that there'll be time for any," he grunted.

"Well, the boss did say the guys up here assured him they would make us feel at home with their New England hospitality," said Kevin.

"Let's get in there and see if they're telling the truth," cried Matt, as he jumped out of the car.

Once inside, they were greeted by a young hotel clerk. "Hello," Matt said. We're with the Utility Workers Union. Can you please help us with our reservations?" he asked.

"I'll be glad to assist you," she answered.

"Thank you kindly," answered Matt. "My name is Matthew Reilly and this is my buddy Kevin Gillen."

"Yes, I see your names here," she said looking at her list. "I have you both assigned to room 12. I'm sorry but as you must know our elevators aren't working since we have no power. You can take the main staircase one flight up and to your right. Your room is at the end of the hall on your left."

The two men had already noticed that their temporary abode had not gone unscathed by the storm. The clerk advised them that there was no telephone service or electricity available, and that the storm had destroyed some of the local cell phone towers. On the other hand, the owners had made many provisions for their comfort. The rooms were well lit with large hurricane oil lamps, and there were fireplaces in each of the sitting rooms. The hotel was improvising as best it could with temporary refrigeration, dry ice, and coolers. There were also plenty of battery-operated flashlights and lanterns. The owners had definitely gone out of their way to compensate for any inconvenience.

Matt and Kevin inquired about their co-workers and were informed that they had checked in already and had left for the union hall. The hall was established as the temporary headquarters for this operation in order to accommodate and organize the many out-of-towners.

"Thank you so much for all of your help," Matt said as Kevin nodded shyly in agreement.

"You are very welcome, Mr. Reilly," the pretty girl answered.

"Please call me Matt," he said as he smiled.

"We have two hours before the briefing session begins so they can give all of us training advice and our assignments," said Matt. "Why don't we get settled in our room and freshen up first before we head out?"

"Fine with me," agreed Kevin as he began to lift his travel bag and start for the stairs.

"The girl at the desk is a real babe, huh Kev? We'll have to check her out later." Kevin was so shocked at Matt's unexpected remark that he couldn't answer. From what Kevin knew of him, Matt had the reputation of being the epitome of a gentleman. Rumor also had it that Matt was a happily married man with a beautiful wife and an adorable daughter. What more could a man want, thought Kevin.

MONDAY, OCTOBER 3, LATER

The union hall was extremely well organized although it was very crowded with utility workers and electricians from different union locals in the tri-state area from New York, New Jersey, and Connecticut. Public pressure was on to restore power as soon as possible, but progress would be slow since the main power plant was incapacitated by the storm and would have to be reconstructed. The nor'easter had been one of the worst storms to hit the area in years. Matt and Kevin learned that many residents of Litchfield, as well as surrounding areas, would have to endure the inconvenience of the power outage, some longer than others. The devastation was extremely sporadic depending on the power that supplied each area. Many of the outages were caused by fallen trees that ripped down power lines and transformers.

There were labelled tables set up along the periphery of the large room for the guys to register. Then they were given their foreman's name and table number to report to. The men were immediately sent out to the field to start work. Matt found that he and his co-workers from Jersey were assigned to different foremen. Matt was happy to find that he would be working with different guys since it gave him the opportunity to get a feel for the area. Matt's foreman, Jack, was a fair and hard-working boss, but he had a reputation for playing hard too. He was one of the most respected men in the local.

Jack and Matt took an instant liking to each other. Matt was teamed up with two guys much younger than he was, Billy and Tommy. The two were a cross between Abbott and Costello or Ralph Kramden and Ed Norton. They were quite comical but great guys to work with. Before the three of them set out, Matt told Kevin that he would meet him back at their B & B where they could compare notes on the day. They wished each other well until later.

Matt could not believe the damage the storm had created. This would not be a case of just flipping a switch or replacing a part to restore service. This required planning from scratch and rebuilding. Telephone poles with their lines were cracked and down everywhere. Matt and his teammates began moving to their designated area and first took inventory of what they could repair, as opposed to what needed to be ordered, such as new poles or lines. Flood waters made the crisis even worse, keeping them from certain damaged areas for fear of electrocution and greatly hindering the restoration process. The work was definitely going to take four weeks at the very least.

They worked into the night before Jack called one of the fellas and told him that it was a wrap for the day. He said he was going to the Sahara Bar if they wanted to meet him there and if Matt was interested to bring him too. Matt was more than happy to go along and observed that Jack and his crew must be regular customers at the Sahara from the way they were greeted by their first names.

"So, Matt, how did it go today?" Jack asked, as he came up from behind him. Matt just shook his head in disbelief.

"The devastation is surreal."

"That's why *you* are here," Jack said. "Hey, Dennis, would you please get our friend Matt a drink?"

"What'll it be for you?" asked Dennis.

"I'll take vodka on the rocks, no fruit please," answered Matt. They decided to eat dinner there, and Jack agreed to pick up the tab.

Matt immediately took to this place. It was a small bar restaurant with an intimate, cozy atmosphere. The bar area was more like a lounge set off from the main dining room. The bar itself had a semi-circular design and was constructed of dark pine with a brass rail around its outer rim that served as an arm rest for the drinkers. Mirrors behind the bar were smoke-etched with the name Sahara in the center and the various bottles of liquor neatly lined on the shelves on both sides further accented it. In addition, there were several low wooden bistro tables with cushioned chairs on wheels matching the height of the tables for patrons who preferred a more private setting. Lit candles on every table added to the ambiance while the dimness made it the perfect place for romance, thought Matt.

The men chatted at the bar while they waited for their food. It wasn't too long until a capable waitress carrying a slew of heavy plates approached them. She was an attractive woman with auburn hair and hazel brown eyes and had a vivacious personality.

"Okay, gentlemen, who is having the prime rib medium?" she asked. No one answered as she tried to hold onto the heavy plates.

"Didn't you order that?" said Tommy to Matt.

"What? Oh yeah! I'm sorry; I did order that." He was blatantly staring at the poor waitress, who was trying to balance the awkward plates.

"That's alright," she said as she placed his meal in front of him, "as long as you enjoy your meal."

After the waitress had delivered all the men's meals, and she was about to walk away, Jack called her back over. He couldn't help but notice Matt's interest in her.

"Julie, I'd like you to meet Matt; he's from Jersey, and he'll be helping us out for a while."

"Hello, Matt. I hope you like it up here, but you may want to watch the company you keep. This is a wild bunch." The group began to laugh.

Matt stood and extended his hand to her and said, "I'm glad to meet you. Would you like to join us for a drink when you're finished?"

"Maybe I will," she said. "Let me just do my side work and I'll be right over."

In the meantime, Matt's cell phone began to ring.

"I thought there was no cell service in this area," he said in surprise.

"Here there is," claimed Tommy, "but you can go up the street or around the corner and there won't be any."

Matt answered his phone to Katie.

"Please hold on, while I go outside," Matt said to her, adding "Excuse me, guys, I'll be right back," as he walked toward the door.

Once outside he said, "Hi Katie."

"Matt, are you alright? Where have you been?" a concerned Katie asked. "Why didn't you call me to let me know you that arrived there okay?"

"Please calm down, honey; I'm just fine," he assured her. "The cell service is crazy up here. It works on one street and not on the next. It has a mind of its own for the time being. We don't have any land or cell service at the hotel. You wouldn't believe the mess up here," he said and proceeded to describe the devastation. "We just got off work and are grabbing something to eat," he told her.

"How's your hotel?" she asked still annoyed.

"We don't have any electricity, but it's okay. We have oil lamps," he said.

"Laura went to bed whining because you didn't call her. She said you promised to call her every night," Katie reminded him.

"Is she still up?" he asked.

"No, she's been sleeping for a while now, but tomorrow first thing I'll explain the cell situation to her. I miss you already."

"Same here, listen, I'd better get back inside; my boss is buying dinner tonight. I'll call as soon as I can. I don't want you to worry; just know that I love you," he reassured her again.

When Matt returned to the bar, he was happy to find that Julie had taken a seat next to his.

"I'm sorry," he apologized to the group as he sat.

"Not a problem," said Julie. "Your wife must be worried."

"I'm not married," he quickly said.

"It's hard to believe a good-looking fella like you hasn't been snatched up already!" replied Julie, and then glanced at his hand to see that he wasn't wearing a wedding ring.

"Nope," said Matt. "I'm not sure if I believe that we are meant to spend our lives with only one person. It seems unnatural to me."

"I think animals are programmed to live with multiple partners, not humans," she opined.

"You may be right," Matt replied. "Maybe I just haven't met the right one yet." Upon hearing this, Julie's heart just skipped a beat. He was such a hunk; how lucky could a girl get, she thought.

"So, what about you?" asked Matt "Are you married?"

"No, not anymore," she sighed.

"What happened, if you don't mind me asking?"

"Caught him with someone and filed for divorce the next day."

"He let you go just like that!"

"Well, not before the countless 'I'm sorries,' not to mention the usual lines: 'It didn't mean anything,' 'I'll never do it again,' and 'You're the only one I love.'"

"Wow, the poor guy; no mercy, huh? Maybe he meant what he said."

"In that case, I guess he should have thought more before he did it. He literally broke my heart. Maybe we were just meant to be best friends and that is all."

"Oh, so you're still in contact with him?"

"He's a great friend, but a lousy husband."

"Any kids?"

"No, that's my biggest regret. I love children," she said sadly.

"Hey, Matt, ready to go?" Jack asked loudly. "We have to be back on the job at six in the morning."

"I guess so!" Matt replied.

With that, Matt turned to Julie as he rose from his bar stool and asked if she would be working the following night. He assured her that he would ask Jack to bring him by for a drink.

She smiled at him demurely as she watched him reach across the bar to shake hands with Dennis.

"It was nice to meet you. Maybe I'll see you again soon."

"The pleasure is mutual," answered Dennis. "I hope you enjoy your stay here."

"I'm sure I'll see you again," Matt said as he winked at Julie. Their immediate attraction to each other was obvious to Dennis.

"I hate to break this party up but I have to get our guest back to his hotel so he can get a couple of winks before I have him back on the chain gang in the morning," Jack said. "I think you guys could also use some zzz's."

"When the boss speaks, we all listen," said Tommy, as he stood up to leave. The good nights passed back and forth among the group. Then they all shouted in unison,

"Bye Dennis! Bye Julie! See you tomorrow."

"Can't wait," quipped Julie facetiously as they all left.

As Julie helped Dennis clean up, he asked her, "Nice guy, that Matt, huh?"

"Too nice," she answered, then added, "he's almost too good to be true!"

"Well, if you feel that way just take it slow. You've been down that road before. I'm surprised that you are not your sceptical self with this guy. He is in his early to mid-thirties, not married according to him, and no immediate family ties."

"I don't know: he evidently has his reasons. I have a strong feeling that he is different than most guys," she said.

"Maybe because you want him to be different because you're lonely," he gently warned her.

"See you tomorrow, Dennis," she responded ignoring his last comment.

"Sure. Thanks for helping me close up," he said. "Safe home, Julie, and I'll see you tomorrow." Despite the busy night they'd had, Dennis noticed that Julie had a little extra spring in her step as she made her way out to the parking lot.

Dennis thought the world of Julie. He considered her to be one of the strongest, yet warmest and most generous people he had ever met. She was always willing to help any-one in need. He sensed how lonely she was at the young age of thirty-three. Dennis always hoped that Julie would take another chance at love. Unfortunately, she had lost faith in men after her divorce from David and hadn't dated since. In fact, from what Dennis knew, David was her first and only love. Dennis constantly tried to persuade her to give love another chance when some nice man pursued her, but she always shied away. Dennis was hoping this guy Matt, might be the one to put a spark back into Julie's love life.

TUESDAY, OCTOBER 4

Matt awoke to Kevin's stealthy movements around their room.

"How long have you been awake," asked Matt?

"Long enough to shower and dress," Kevin answered.

You were asleep when I got in," said Matt.

"Yeah, I was beat and went out like a light. By the way, did you leave that kerosene lamp on all night?"

"I must have. I'm so sorry about that. I dropped into bed without noticing that it was on," Matt lied nonchalantly. "I should have known better. How did your first day go," Matt asked changing the subject?

The guys are okay. The work is the same no matter where it is. Foreman wants to get the work done and get back to a regular schedule. I'd rather be home in my own routine anyway."

Matt responded, "I'm trying to make the best of it myself. I try to make an adventure out of every experience and that helps the time to pass faster for me. I think I'll jump in the shower now and meet you downstairs for breakfast. Can't wait to see what they can conjure up without electricity. Jack is picking me up just before six."

"It sounds like you're in good with the foreman. Not bad, though I'm not surprised."

Matt wasn't sure how to take that last remark, so he just ignored it and responded, "He's just a really great boss. All the guys love him. He took me to dinner last night with the rest of the guys. He takes good care of his men."

"Glad to hear you lucked out. By the way, it's pouring outside. Working is going to be a nightmare today," said Kevin.

"Great, just what we need, more water to deal with. I wonder if we'll work a full day," offered Matt.

"Um, that's a thought," mused Kevin. "I'll see you downstairs."

Matt had just about finished his coffee and donut when Jack pulled up in front of the hotel. He jumped up and bid Kevin good-bye.

"Maybe I'll see you tonight if you're up when I get in later. The guys were talking about going out for a bite again after work." Kevin just looked after Matt as he ran through the rain to Jack's SUV, wondering if he had been wrong about him all this time. Something about Matt was not quite right, but he just couldn't put his finger on it.

The work day crept along, and Matt was counting the hours as they passed. Nothing went smoothly, and the working conditions were horrendous and very dangerous. A lot of power poles were down and wires were hanging, electrifying anything they came into contact with. Several local substations were making extremely slow progress in restoring its own power, which hindered the work of the outside linemen. The many areas that were flooded and the additional rain water added to the overall frustration.

It was two o'clock when Jack called it a day, and the fellows couldn't get to the Sahara fast enough. They welcomed a cold beer and a hot lunch to compensate for their long difficult endeavors.

The men dashed into the Sahara like four drenched rats seeking refuge from the torrential rains at their backs. Once inside the bar, they quickly removed their soaked clothing and rain gear, shaking the water from them without realizing they were spritzing Dennis with the excess.

"Hey if I wanted a shower, I'd stand outside," Dennis complained good-naturedly.

"Sorry Dennis, we just wanted to get these wet things off," apologized Matt for the group.

"I feel like I've just been sprinkled by the gods of mischief," said Dennis as he dried himself off with a bar rag.

"Now that's a title I like," said Billy, as he took his usual seat at the bar.

"I feel more like a soaked sponge than a god," moaned Tommy.

"Are you guys finished for the day or just having lunch?" asked Dennis.

"We can't accomplish anything more out there today," said a disappointed Jack. "We'll just have to make up for it tomorrow."

"Ugh," the other fellows chimed in unison.

Matt was lost in his own thoughts as he looked around the bar and restaurant like a lighthouse beam circling in search of a missing ship.

"Ahem," sounded Dennis as he stood waiting for Matt's attention. He repeated, "Vodka rocks, no olive?"

"Oh, I'm sorry Dennis, I didn't hear you. Yes, that's right."

As if reading Matt's mind, Dennis nonchalantly mentioned that Julie was leaving early to help two of their regular customers, Marilyn and her sister Maggie, whose basement was flooded with three feet of water. Dennis offered to cover for Julie if any customers should come in.

"Okay Dennis, I'm leaving," Julie announced as she hurried into the lounge unaware of the guys sitting at the bar.

"Oh, hi fellas, you're in early today. Is this a slack break or are you finished for the day?" she asked.

"It's more like Mother Nature giving us time off for good behavior," boasted Tommy.

"Dennis, do you want me to wait and serve their food before I leave?" Julie asked.

"No, go ahead. If you wait any longer, you'll need a lifeboat to rescue Marilyn and Maggie," said Dennis.

Before anyone could comment, Matt was standing putting his wet coat back on. "I'll go with you," he offered. "I'm sure you ladies can use my help."

"Well, wait until we grab a bite and we'll help too. We'll have them bailed out in no time," insisted Billy.

"I'll go ahead with Julie and you guys can catch up with us after you've eaten," suggested Matt.

"Take a couple of pails out of the truck and we'll bring along the rest," said Jack.

"You fellas are the best," cried Julie.

"For you Julie, anything," said Jack sincerely. "We're also fond of those two damsels in distress. They're great people."

"They sure are," agreed Billy. "They throw the best St. Patty's Day party ever."

"Matt, we'll bring you the lunch special of the day," said Jack realizing that Matt hadn't eaten yet.

"Thanks, Jack. See you in a while," he said as he hurried to catch up with Julie who was already out the door.

Marilyn and Maggie were in a bad state when Julie and Matt arrived. They were obviously exhausted from trying to keep up with the flooding but the rain just poured in faster than they could bail it out. It was with Matt's ingenuity that they were able to siphon the water out to the street through two garden hoses.

The rest of the rescue team arrived and "Project Damsels" began just as the rain subsided. An assembly line was organized with Jack, Billy, and Tommy passing pails full of water out the basement window to Matt and Julie to dump. Marilyn and Maggie then returned the empty pails back to the basement crew. The tedious process continued for three hours until it was agreed that residual water could be handled by their Dri-Vac. The work team was exhausted as well as soaked. The grateful hostesses were happy to provide dry towels and soothing hot toddies for everyone.

The sisters were enchanted by Matt's charm and good nature. Either of them wouldn't have minded meeting him before Julie. They immediately recognized the chemistry between the two and were happy for her. They had known how empty her life had been and could see a powerful change in Julie while in the presence of Matt; both wondered what the future would hold for her. They considered her to be one of the sweetest and most generous people they were graced to know. She had offered for them to stay with her until their electricity came back on, yet they had decided to tough it out for the past week and were relieved when their power was finally restored. Marilyn and Maggie bid goodbye to the five heroes and promised to see them soon at the Sahara.

Matt made it a point to impress Julie by opening the car door for her when he slipped and fell into a huge mud puddle. She did everything to keep from splitting a gut with the others, but the scene was just too hilarious. She offered her hand to help him up when he yanked it and pulled her into the misery with him. They convulsed in laughter as they rolled in the sludge. Matt impulsively pulled her to him and kissed her. Julie immediately jumped up.

"I'm sorry. I couldn't help it," Matt apologized.

"It's okay," Julie answered a bit dazed. "I wasn't expecting that."

The two stood mirroring each other's muddy appearance and again broke into laughter. Julie was relieved to find an old beach blanket in her trunk to protect her car's interior. Jack agreed to give the other muddy mess a ride to his hotel.

After a nice hot shower and his now cold lunch, Matt dared not venture out again. Kevin hadn't returned to the room yet. Matt was exhausted from the day's activities and fell asleep, but not before he tried to call Katie hoping his cell might be able to pick up a signal. It was not to be, leaving him with no one to share his crazy day's adventure.

WEDNESDAY, OCTOBER 5

Julie awoke to a new sunny day. Matt had removed the clouds from her sky, and now her horizons seemed endless. Just a few days ago her life was lonely and gray. Matt had brought a new excitement to her existence. He was a natural gentleman, the last of a generation long gone. She was hoping to see him tonight especially after thinking about his spontaneous kiss from the day before. The memory lingered throughout her day as she chuckled at the muddy messes they had been.

She wanted to stay focused but each thought of him made her head spin. She promised herself to take one day at a time. Take it slow, she told herself, you've had enough heartache for a lifetime.

Besides, his stay is only temporary. She was determined to enjoy every minute as long as it lasted, maybe forever. Anything was possible; *things are happening every day*, she thought. Well, wasn't that what the Fairy Godmother told Cinderella?

Julie spent her day drifting in and out of her fairy tale reverie. It was certainly more satisfying than her usual habit of dissecting reality. She couldn't wait to get to work later and wait for Matt to appear.

"Here they come! The starving stampede of bulls!" laughed Julie, as they charged in past her to claim their seats at the bar. Dennis, a well-seasoned bartender, had their beers and Matt's vodka ready before they were even seated.

"Oh, Dennis, you are the best! Keep 'em coming!" exclaimed Billy.

"Sounds like you had another rough day, guys," said Dennis.

"You can say that again," replied Billy.

Tommy was quick to add, "Helping Marilyn and Maggie yesterday was fun compared to today's labor."

"C'mon, fellas, you'll have our New Jersey visitor thinking you're a bunch of wimps," quipped Jack.

"Oh no, Jack, I have to agree with them. Anything that could have gone wrong today, went wrong," affirmed Matt.

Standing next to Matt, Julie announced, "Fellas, you're a bit late tonight, but the kitchen agreed to stay open until you're served."

"I'll take your orders as soon as you're ready," said Dennis.

Matt turned to Julie and asked her to join them when she got off. She gladly agreed to do so.

After the food was delivered, Matt asked Julie to move with him to a private lounge table. He carried their drinks, while she transferred his dinner. The small bistro table stood in the corner of the bar well out of earshot of the other guys. There were no other patrons in the restaurant or bar except for the electrical workers.

"I was looking forward to seeing you tonight," said Matt as he graciously pulled out the chair for her.

"Thank you," said Julie. "I'm glad somebody was."

"Oh, c'mon, I'm sure a lot of men find you attractive."

"Really?" she asked. "Where are they?"

"I'm right here, and right now that's all that matters," he whispered as he stared intently into her eyes.

"I guess I'm not actually used to taking compliments," she answered.

"Well, I hope you can get used to it, 'cause you are going to hear plenty from me. Seriously, I like you. I felt an immediate connection when I met you. I can't explain it," he said.

"That's strange because I was feeling the same way when I saw you," she told him.

With each sip of their drinks, they became more and more enchanted with each other. It wasn't long before they began melting into each other, and small pecks on the lips became long hungry kisses. She asked him about his roommate and their accommodations at their hotel with the lack of modern conveniences. He told her about Kevin being a reserved kind of guy, and that their breakfast consisted of coffee and donuts imported from another area with power.

Julie mused for a minute and then asked Matt, "I don't want to sound forward or anything, but I have a three-bedroom house in a nearby town with all the comforts of home, including electricity. Why don't you stay with me while you're here? The area where I live hasn't lost power." She asked out of genuine kindness.

Matt looked longingly at her, but answered, "You don't have to do that. I really don't want to put you out like that."

"You wouldn't be putting me out," she said as she went on. "It's only temporary, and I surely wouldn't mind some company. And by the way, I make the best hot buttery pancakes around."

"They're my favorite. I guess I can't turn down an offer like that as long as we seal it with a kiss," he whispered, as he leaned in and kissed her fervently on the lips.

"I can take you over to your hotel to get your things before I take you to my place," she said.

"That sounds great! You know, you truly are a wonderful person," he responded. They gathered their things and made their way to the bar, where Matt paid the check. Matt made sure he was very discreet when he told Jack the plans so the other guys wouldn't overhear. He was delighted when Jack offered to still pick him up in the mornings on his way to work. Boy, this New England hospitality is really something, Matt thought to himself. He and Julie tried to make a subtle exit with a general good night to all.

Julie had to remind Matt that they had an agenda as he covered her mouth with his passionate kisses.

"We'll never get you home and settled if we don't get this car started and get over to your hotel to get your things," she gasped, her heart skipping. He made her feel like a teenager again and a very desirable woman at the same time. She had almost forgotten such feelings existed.

It wasn't long before they were at her house unpacking his things. He had scooted in and out of the hotel after leaving a note for Kevin who was dead asleep, unaware that Matt was even there. He explained that he would be staying with a friend of Jack's and couldn't pass up the offer of home-cooked meals. He certainly didn't want to infer that the friend was a woman. Matt was also sure that Kevin would appreciate having the room to himself.

Matt was impressed with Julie's beautiful house. He turned his concentration back to his hostess sitting beside him on the couch. "You have a beautiful home here."

"Thank you, David gave it to me as part of the divorce agreement as well as half of all our assets. I guess he thought it was a way of relieving his guilt." Matt looked a bit puzzled. As though she was reading his mind, she explained, "I only waitress to keep busy and to get out of the house. I like the flexible schedule and it gives me the opportunity to meet interesting people, present company included." Her resilience and strength fascinated him. Plus, she was a very attractive woman. She cuddled into him, scarcely believing that she could feel so comfortable with a stranger she hardly knew, but to whom she felt so closely connected.

"You must be exhausted," she said. "I have your room ready. If you need anything, just give a shout. Your wish is my command. I sincerely want you to feel comfortable while you're here."

He kissed the tip of her nose and asked, "Can I sleep with you? I don't like to sleep alone. I'm afraid of the dark." His plea sounded like one of a little boy who was trying to charm someone into giving him his own way. She was amused by his friskiness with no inkling that he could possibly be serious.

Before she could respond, he pulled her into his arms as his hands and mouth explored the curves of her body. She lost all sense of time or place as they rolled onto the floor, and he mounted her with rhythmic thrusts as they kissed and panted until, finally, they both climaxed and collapsed onto each other. She felt exhilaration like never before. He stood and extended his hand to help her up onto her wobbling legs. Without a word, he carried her up the stairs and into the bedroom where their lovemaking continued into the morning. Julie felt an intimacy with Matt that she had never experienced with anyone else. It felt so right. He had to be her destiny. What were the chances of meeting a great looking single gentleman with no kids and a great job? She felt like the luckiest woman in the world and pondered whether Matt had entered her life "for a reason, a season, or a lifetime," as she had read in a recent e-mail. Only time would tell.

THURSDAY, OCTOBER 6

Matt considered himself lucky when he awoke to the smell of brewing coffee, bacon, eggs, and the buttery pancakes he had been promised. He quickly made his way to the kitchen to find Julie placing his full plate on the table. He whirled her around and kissed her passionately.

"I thought I'd died and gone to heaven when I smelled these goodies," said Matt.

"I hope you enjoy them. I'm not working tonight; maybe we can do something," suggested Julie. "That would be great," he answered, "but I don't know what time I'll be home. I'll try to call you if I can, but you know how unreliable the cell service is."

"That's okay; no call is necessary. I'll just wait for you."

Matt complimented Julie on her cooking and blew her a kiss. He jumped up and ran to take a shower since Jack would be there to pick him up any minute. He was hoping he would have a minute to call to say hello to Laura.

Ten minutes later he was showered and dressed and downstairs kissing Julie good-bye. He told her he was going to wait outside for Jack and looked forward to seeing her later that night. A few moments later she peeked out the window to see him on his cell phone and wondered who he could be talking to this early in the morning.

Matt was pacing back and forth on the street as he spoke on his cell. "Good morning, Katie! Surprise, I think that I've found a cell signal area. I know it's early but I never know when I'll be able to call you. I may be able to call around this time every morning. So, how are my two favorite ladies doing?"

"We're doing okay, but we miss you. That's a great relief that we'll be able to keep in touch every day."

"Before I forget, on the ride up here I had a great idea! What about setting up Kevin with Ann Marie? I know that you don't know him, but he's a good guy, and, well, we both just love Ann Marie! Wouldn't it be great if we could go out again as a foursome?" he tried to convince her.

"It's something to think about, but let's talk more about it when you get home. Okay, hon?" she asked, then added, "When will you be coming home this weekend?"

"I'm afraid there's no way. You wouldn't believe the work up here."

"You can't be serious! Matt, I thought the arrangement was that you would be home every weekend!"

"Katie, haven't you been following the news about the devastation up here?"

"I don't care! That's not what you told me! I would never had agreed to your volunteering to work up there, if you weren't coming home every weekend!"

"What do you think? That this is fun for me! Not only am I exhausted but also my whole body aches!"

"I'm sorry. I just don't know if the extra money is worth us being separated. My poor honey. If you were home I would give you a nice back rub while I whispered dirty thoughts in your ears," she teased.

"Oh, baby, don't do that to me. You're getting me all worked up. I want a rain check for when I get home."

"You bet! Laura just woke up; so you can talk to her now."

"Hey, guess who is on the phone for you, Laura?" Katie said.

"Hi Daddy," Laura cried. "I miss you too much."

"I miss you, too, honey. Did Mommy tell you about the cell phone problem up here? I promise I'll call you whenever I can, but you have to remember how much I love you."

"When are you coming home?" she asked in excitement.

"Maybe next weekend, depending on what my boss says.

"But that's not fair, Daddy! You said you'd be home every weekend!

"Honey I can't help it! There are so many people up here that don't have electricity. They can't watch T.V. or cook," he said appealing to her little heart. "Okay for this time, *only*! Oh, I almost forgot to tell you about my new pet Mommy bought for me. It's a chameleon. Do you know what that is, Daddy? It's a lizard who changes its color to match wherever he lives. Daddy, I named him Mattie after you, 'cause I love him just like you. I'm gonna' go see him now, so you can talk to Mommy. I love you, Daddy."

He responded with, "I love you, too, baby."

Just then Jack pulled up, and Matt quickly said good-bye to Katie and assured her he loved her and would call again as soon as he got the chance.

Once Matt was in the car, Jack asked him how last night's move into Julie's house had gone. "I'm glad to hear you're comfortable. Julie is a real doll and a very nice person, but please be careful; she has been through a lot."

"You don't have to worry, Jack; Julie is a grown woman and a very beautiful one at that. We've both agreed to enjoy our temporary arrangement."

Jack was happy that Julie had agreed to the ground rules from the start. She needed a little excitement in her life anyway, Jack thought to himself; he just hoped Matt wasn't too much of that for her. Suddenly, Matt's cell phone rang, temporarily saving him from any further warnings from Jack.

"Hi, Kev. I see you found my note. I didn't want to wake you up, knowing how you need your beauty sleep," he chuckled. "I don't know if I'll be going home this weekend. It depends on how tired I am, and seeing that it's really only for one day, the last thing I want to do is to spend it traveling. I'll let you know tomorrow for sure. Thanks, buddy. Take care and I'll talk to you tomorrow." As he hung up he turned to Jack and said, "That Kevin, you couldn't find a nicer guy."

Julie kept busy throughout the day, constantly pinching herself to be sure she wasn't dreaming about the gorgeous man she had slept with the night before. The doorbell interrupted her thoughts, and she found a subtly handsome man at her door when she opened it.

"I'm glad to catch you home," he said.

"What brings you by, David?" she asked.

"I just wanted to be sure you were okay after that terrible storm," he answered.

""I can assure you that I am better than ever. I guess you're looking to come in," she said in a sarcastic tone as she held the door open and waved him in.

David sensed a change in Julie and was interested in finding out what it was. "Anything new with you?" he asked.

"Funny you should ask, but yes, there is," she replied. "I met the most wonderful man in the world."

"Oh, you mean I'm not?"

"You lost that title a long time ago."

"I'll never stop trying to win it back."

"Oh David, can't you just be happy with our friendship?"

"You can't keep me from trying."

"In that case, I won't tell you about my new love," she teased.

"Oh, please do; I am just dying to hear," he said facetiously.

When she told him she had invited Matt to live with her after only knowing him for only a few days, he was floored. "What are you thinking, Julie?" he asked. "He could be a murderer or a con man. I can't believe you could do something so crazy."

She turned around and pointed to the door. "David, if you're not happy with being my dearest friend and trusting my judgment, you can leave right now. You no longer have the right to question my decisions. You gave that right away five years ago."

He knew if he continued berating her, she would only push him away. And *that* he would not be able to handle. He needed her in his life, but he also wanted her to be safe.

"I am truly sorry, Julie," he said calmly. "It's just that I worry about you. And yes, I do treasure our friendship. Please go ahead and tell me about this guy." He sat and listened with a heavy heart as Julie described her new love and how she met him. She made it sound as though this guy could walk on air as if he were Mr. Perfect. It hurt to think she had once thought of him that way before he had blown it with that office floozy. That moment of weakness had cost him his wife, and he would do anything to win her back even if it meant listening to her talk about this Casanova. He stopped her from relating any of the intimate details because he couldn't bear to hear it. At least this guy would be staying only a month, he thought, and I'll be here to apply the Band-Aid to her heart when the guy leaves.

"So when do I get to meet your new beau?" he asked.

"I really can't say right now with his long work hours, but maybe when things settle down I'll call you," she answered.

"That would be fine. I really am happy for you and I hope it works out," he lied. "Please keep in touch and let me know how things are going for you. I really do care." David gave her a big kiss on the cheek as he hugged her good-bye. Tears welled up in his eyes as he walked away from her.

Julie couldn't help comparing Matt to her ex-husband. David stood just about six feet with curly brown hair and beautiful hazel eyes, while Matt's darker brown hair contrasted with his sparkling brown eyes. Although he was handsome, David did not possess the magnetism that Matt did. People were attracted to Matt's Irish warmth and easy personality while David, although also of Celtic descent was more reserved.

After David had left, Julie thoughts reverted back to her new Prince Charming. She had at first had the same suspicions about Matt that David had just expressed but she was able to rule them out by the way he treated her as well as by his interaction with her friends and other people. She started concentrating on what they would do that evening. She decided to make an exceptional dinner and leave the recreation up to him. She had not felt this desirable and beautiful in a long time. She thought, could this really be a Cinderella experience for me?

As Matt entered the house after work, he was greeted by an enticing aroma emanating from the kitchen. He immediately followed the scent, and Julie turned to greet him with a kiss as she handed him a glass of wine. She was dressed in a short black skirt with a low-cut sparkling blue blouse that showed off her cleavage as well as her auburn hair and hazel eyes. She was wearing a white lace apron to protect her clothes and was standing in bare feet. She looked like a sexy Donna Reed greeting her husband after a hard day's work.

Now it was Matt who was weak in the knees, and he couldn't keep his eyes or hands off her.

"Oh, baby," he moaned as he groped her ferociously, causing her to put down their wine glasses. His mouth was all over her face and mouth as he groaned, "How long until dinner?" Julie managed to murmur "about half an hour," as he lifted a glass of wine, handed it to her, lifted his own, then took her hand and led her to the living room couch.

In no time their clothes littered the living room floor and their bodies were entwined. He masterfully used his mouth and hands to please her in ways she had never experienced before. She moaned into orgasm and then concentrated on him until he exploded in her. They both collapsed onto the floor in pure euphoria.

"Oh my God, you are so good, babe," he muttered. It took a few minutes before either of them could move. He led her to the shower where they playfully washed each other.

"I think I'll go and fix our dinner while you finish up," Julie said. She quickly dried off, wrapped herself in her terry robe, and pinned her hair up loosely. She wanted their dinner to be perfect.

They sat and ate by candlelight with soft music playing. She had prepared filet mignon au poivre, scalloped potatoes, and fresh French string beans sautéed in a light lemon and garlic sauce. It was like an elegant love scene out of an old movie.

"You've really outdone yourself," said Matt.

"I'm glad you like my cooking," she said. "I guess you're too tired to go out tonight."

"Are you kidding? You just revved me up. I wouldn't mind going out for a drink or two." After dinner, they did the dishes together and then got ready to go out.

Matt was delighted when Julie suggested they walk two blocks away to a local pub called Conor's, a very small bar sequestered among other old colonial homes just like Julie's.

Most of the residents, if not all, were patrons of the place and considered it their private club. There was a small patio on the side of the building hidden by a well-manicured row of hedges that kept it very secluded. The building itself resembled a small Tudor cottage, and the interior was just as quaint with dark rustic beams accenting the stucco ceiling and walls that were partially wallpapered in warm Victorian colors of green and dark mauve. The wall sconces and the bevelled bar mirrors added to the Victorian ambience, while the wall-to-wall dark evergreen rug strewn with light mauve designs provided contrast to the room and ensured a welcoming feeling to all who entered.

Allie, the barmaid, was a petite attractive Brazilian girl with long hair that fell in spiral curls. Her twinkling blue eyes entertained her patrons as though she was holding court. Although the bar itself seated no more than twelve people, there were four bistro tables with chairs that comfortably seated the overflow and were close enough so that all could engage in conversation and not feel isolated or left out. Matt and Julie took the seats at the end of the bar as she introduced him to everyone. There was Bobby, Janie, Chris, Anna, Mike, Theresa, and Karly. They were a great group of people who made Matt feel very comfortable, and here, too, Matt fit right in.

Mike suddenly announced to the group, "I found a new BFF. Matt here is a fellow New York Giants fan. Allie, please buy him a drink on me." Their conversation centered on the history of the trials and tribulations of the Giants. Theresa told Julie she was glad that Mike had found another Giants fanatic, so she would be spared listening to him constantly going on about the team. It wasn't long until Bobby and Chris joined the bar stool quarterbacks. Their conversation centered on debating the statistics versus the predictions, as though they were expert sports analysts.

The girls, on the other hand, focused on local gossip, mostly regarding the effects of the storm. They also chatted about the handsome newcomer to their group as a prospective husband for Julie. She downplayed their excitement, however, and said, "Let's not get carried away. I'm just enjoying each minute that we're together for the time being." She didn't want anything or anyone to ruin this magical time for her.

Karly pulled Julie aside and asked if Matt had any single friends for her. Julie laughed and told her he was working with two fellows and suggested that she come into the Sahara one night when Julie was working and she would introduce her to them.

After a couple of rounds of drinks and great conversation, Allie shouted, "last call. Although no one wanted the night to end, they all had to get up in the morning for work, save Julie, who insisted on rising early to make Matt his breakfast. They all said their good-byes and then Matt agreed to meet the guys there for Monday Night Football while waiting for Julie to get home from work. She was happy that he was settling in and making friends.

"I really enjoyed tonight from beginning to end," Matt said, as he lay next to her in bed. He reached over and kissed her. "Thank you so much."

"It was my pleasure," she replied.

"I'll give you pleasure," he growled as he wrestled her into lovemaking.

FRIDAY, OCTOBER 7

By Friday the two lovers were feeling extremely comfortable with each other. Another superb breakfast was ready for Matt again, after a little morning pleasure. Today Julie was bursting with excitement as if she was harboring a secret. She served him his breakfast after planting a playful kiss on his cheek.

"How would you like to spend Sunday in Mystic, Connecticut?" she asked. "I'm off from work, and it is so lovely this time of year. The foliage is breath taking, and the colors are indescribable. It really is so gorgeous here now. Have you ever seen New England in the autumn?"

"No, but it sounds wonderful!" he answered. "But do you think the seaport is open so soon after the storm?" he reminded her.

"I already called and amazingly, the coast was not at all affected. The person I spoke to told me this storm's unusual pattern was so erratic and the destruction mostly occurred inland. I don't remember ever seeing anything like this before."

"I'm so glad the coast wasn't affected. You know, I've wanted to go to Mystic Seaport since I was a kid. I missed my fourth grade class trip there because I was sick. Well, that's not exactly true…actually, my mother couldn't afford for me to go. But of course, I couldn't tell my teacher or my classmates that. I remember them telling me wonderful stories about the trip. I just pretended that I really didn't care. At that time of my childhood, I was fascinated by seafaring sailors and ships. It broke my heart to not be able to go. I know my mom felt bad, but she was as tough as nails and wouldn't let on."

"Oh Matt, that must have been a traumatic ordeal for you at the time," she said sympathetically.

"No worse than all the other childhood ordeals I experienced. I can't believe that I'm finally going there after all these years," he said. Matt gave her a lingering kiss and hug before lumbering up the stairs like a big child who had just opened a wonderful Christmas gift. After a kiss good-bye, Matt went out front to wait for Jack.

Julie glanced out the window to see him talking on his cell again, walking back and forth. 'Um!' Julie thought, 'Again! *Who is* he talking to at this time of the morning?' Maybe she was just over reacting and it was Jack or one of his co-workers he was talking to.

When Matt heard Katie on the other end, he spoke with his bedroom voice, "Well, hello babe, this is your lonely husband calling to see if you miss me."

"Of course, darling, but I would rather wake up to your voice in my ear lying next to me in bed instead of on the phone."

"Me, too, hon," he sighed.

"Before I forget, I want you to know that Laura and I are going with Ann Marie and Suzie to their summer house in Point Pleasant since it's a three day weekend for Columbus Day. Well, *since* you're not coming home this weekend, I *thought* it might be a good idea for us to get away," she said in a digging manner.

"It is horrible being away from the two of you, but I feel better knowing that you'll be having fun with Ann Marie."

"Yea, yea, yea, we also have a guest coming with us?"

"*Who?*" he questioned, wondering to whom Katie could be referring.

"Mattie!" she cried.

"Mattie who?"

"Laura's chameleon. I guess you forgot! You'll be coming home to a new family member. She refuses to be separated from the creature since it reminds her of you."

"Can you imagine having a chameleon named after you? How many fathers can claim those bragging rights?" he chuckled.

"At least it takes her mind off of your absence, so I guess it's worth the sacrifice. But I warn you that you will be helping her take care of it when you get home. It's really not my cup of tea."

"Don't worry, I will," he said. With that he saw Jack driving up the street toward him, so he said good-bye to Katie. "I'll try to call over the weekend. Be sure to have a great time and give my little girl a kiss for me."

"I will," she said as she hung up. He immediately called Kevin to let him know he definitely wouldn't be going home this weekend.

"Hi Kev," he said. "My wife just called to say the girls are spending the next few days at her best friend's shore house, but I'll probably join you for the ride home next weekend if that is okay. Thanks, Kev. Take it safe, and I'll talk to you soon."

Julie was working a double shift that day at the Sahara, so Matt agreed to stop there after work with Jack, have a drink, and wait for her to finish her shift. Jack was glad to see Julie happy. He had never seen her so content before and wondered how long it would last after Matt left or if they planned on having a long-distance relationship.

When he asked Matt about his intentions for the future, Matt nonchalantly answered, "We're taking it one day at a time," and quickly changed the subject. Jack understood the comment to mean that it was none of his business and promised himself not to get involved. Still, he wasn't sure if it had been such a great idea introducing Matt to Julie. He wouldn't want to be the person responsible for causing any further unhappiness in her life. By the time they made it to the Sahara, Julie was almost finished for the night. She glowed when she saw Matt walk in. She went right up to him and gave him a quick kiss before she went about her business as Matt spotted a chair near Billy and Tommy. The two had managed to get there earlier and were involved in a heated debate over who was going to win the Super Bowl this season, the Giants or the Jets.

Matt easily answered, "The Giants, of course," as he positioned himself between Billy and Tommy. Everyone sitting at the bar broke out in roars of laughter, as Dennis placed Matt's drink in front of him.

"Thanks, Matt, for saving me the trouble of having to referee," Dennis quipped.

"My pleasure," said Matt.

But the entertainment got even better when Tommy took Billy's chair away and sat on it, thinking Billy wasn't using it since he had been standing with his back to him talking to someone for quite a while. Tommy then gave the chair to Matt to save for Julie, so when Billy backed up to sit down, his chair was gone, and his butt landed hard on the floor. The tears were rolling down everyone's cheeks from laughing so hard. The expletives were frothing from Billy's mouth as Tommy tried to explain the situation through his tears.

Julie heard the ruckus coming from the bar and assumed it was football related. She could take or leave football since it wasn't one of her passions, unlike baseball or bowling, for instance. Unfortunately, she couldn't commit to a bowling team with her rotating work schedule, but she did manage to serve as an on-call sub. In fact, the league needed her to sub the next three Wednesdays for a girl who was on her honeymoon. She wondered if Matt happened to bowl also and made a mental note that she must ask him when she told him about that commitment.

SATURDAY, OCTOBER 8

Over breakfast, Julie told Matt about her bowling commitment for the next few Wednesdays. He got excited and asked her if the league needed another sub.

"I'm a sanctioned bowler in a league at home with a decent average, and I have my ABC card with me." She was really thrilled and agreed to call the league president to see if Matt could sub with her Wednesday night. That would be perfect, even if they weren't on the same team since they would still be able to enjoy a night out together under the same roof. Simultaneously, Matt was hoping that Katie remembered to get bowling subs for them while he was away.

While he was waiting for Jack, Matt made his morning call to Katie. "Good morning, darling," he said as she answered with a meek, sleepy "Hi Matt."

"Baby, I'm sorry I woke you. Do you want me to call you later or tomorrow?"

"Oh no, it's okay," she said. "I was just about to get up and join Ann Marie for a cup of coffee out on the terrace." Katie didn't want to miss the chance to talk to him because of the unpredictable cell service in Connecticut.

"How are my girls doing?" he asked.

"We're fine, but I'm still not happy you couldn't be with us this weekend."

"Honey, please, it's not easy on me either. I'm the one here alone."

"Point Pleasant is so beautiful. We've been eating our meals out on the sun porch overlooking the ocean. It would be so romantic with the right person," she hinted.

"Oh, what am I: a bloody substitute?" Ann Marie jested in the background. "Hi Matt," she shouted down the phone. "We're enjoying our girl bonding weekend!"

"Katie, please give my regards to Ann Marie and be sure to thank her for me," Matt spoke sincerely. He was truly grateful that Katie had Ann Marie for companionship while he was away.

"I will. I'd love for us to have a shore house like this some-day," Katie responded.

"Let's work on getting our first house in Hoboken," he said.

"I know, just dreaming. It's the euphoric effect from the ocean breezes," she sighed.

"How's my Laura doing without me?" he asked.

"Better than me. She's been very busy with Suzie and that chameleon. I'm actually getting used to it. It's so ugly that it's cute. The girls are fascinated by it, so it keeps them entertained for hours at a time. He actually follows them around the house changing his colors as he goes. It's just that every time they call his name, I think of you," she sighed.

"Well, that's not a bad thing. What do you, Ann Marie, and the girls have planned for today?" he asked.

"We're thinking of taking them to visit lighthouses in the area."

"I'd like to do that with you sometime."

"I'll be sure to add that to our bucket list."

"Well, here comes Jack, so I'm off. Give my love to the other girls," he added, as they exchanged "I love you-s" and hung up. He was relieved that Katie was in a better spirits.

Meanwhile, Ann Marie had been sitting

"Hi Jack," Matt said as he got into the car.

"Good morning," Jack answered, and then, a bit casually, he asked, "So how are things going?"

Matt excitedly told him, "Julie is going to see if her bowling league needs another sub for the next couple of Wednesdays."

"Geez, you have more of a social life here than I do," laughed Jack. "You and Julie really are suited for each other." Matt got quiet and looked straight ahead for the rest of the ride, clearly signaling that Julie was not a topic he wished to discuss.

Julie was vacuuming when she answered the phone to David.

"Yes, I am still walking on air, and yes, I am still in love with my Prince Charming," she answered. She was reluctant to broach the subject but she needed to be prepared, so she asked him, "Are you interested in buying this house from me *if* I happen to move?" One of the stipulations of their divorce was that she would offer him first dibs on the house in the event that she sold it.

"Aren't you getting ahead of yourself? You don't even know this guy a month and you're talking about making life changes!" he said annoyed.

She tried to stay calm as she answered him with, "I am not getting ahead of myself. And yes, I know it hasn't been long at all, but in case I do move would you be interested in buying the house? That's all I'm asking. I just want to have things in place if Matt doesn't want to stay here. I'm not asking you for your opinion on anything else. Look, you think about it, and I'll talk to you again," she said as she quickly hung up. He could be so frustrating at times, she thought.

Julie was bursting with excitement to tell Matt that a regular customer of hers had given her two tickets to next Friday night's baseball game between the Boston Red Sox and the New York Yankees. It was game two of the playoffs and was being played at Boston's Fenway Park. The irony was that she was a Sox fan and Matt, a diehard Yankee fan, and of course, the two teams have had a long-standing rivalry. She had been to Fenway Park many times with her grandfather and treasured those fond memories. Every year during baseball season he would surprise her with a different team jersey or T-shirt, and she wore it proudly. She wondered if any of those shirts would fit her now. On the other hand, she thought she might just go to a local sports store and buy shirts for herself and Matt along with matching baseball caps. The only problem would be the need for Matt to get off work early since Boston was over two hours away and the game started at seven. They would also have to take into consideration Boston's Friday commuter traffic.

She was tending to one of her dinner tables when Matt came into the Sahara with Jack and took a seat at the bar. She saw him out of the corner of her eye but she was in the middle of taking a dinner order. As soon as she had her customers organized, she dashed over to Matt,

"Guess what! You are never gonna believe what I have for us!" she exclaimed.

"Don't I get a kiss first?" he asked.

She quickly gave him a peck on the cheek and continued, "We have tickets for next Friday night for the Red Sox-Yankees playoff game! *And* they are field box seats between home and third! What do you think of that?"

"How did you ever manage something like that?" he asked, obviously in shock.

"Wow!" jumped in Jack. "I want to go!"

"Sorry, Jack, there's only two tickets," she told him. She quickly tried to explain the story of how her favorite customer, Mr. Reynolds, had given her the tickets, but before she could finish, she had to run off and check on her tables now that the restaurant was getting busy.

Not long after that Julie sat on a bar stool next to Matt that he had saved for her and joined in the playful banter. She then turned to Matt saying, "You wouldn't believe what happened here tonight."

Dennis chimed in, "Julie's night certainly wasn't uneventful."

She went on with her story, "A lovely couple came in for dinner and seemed to be enjoying themselves until I saw the girl take her glass full of red wine and throw it in the guy's face."

Matt asked, "What would make her do something like that?"

"What a mess!" Dennis commented.

Julie continued the story, "He stormed out and left her sobbing. When I went over to clean the table, she told me that her boyfriend of five years had just told her that he met someone new who he was madly in love with and planned to marry. She was heartbroken and never saw it coming. She had to call someone for a ride home. How could somebody do something like that to somebody else?" she asked Matt. He didn't answer but quickly turned back toward Billy as though he had been following his conversation with the others.

"OK," said Tommy loudly, "Who was the greatest quarterback of all time?"

Dennis looked at Matt and Julie, shrugged his shoulders and said, "Here we go again," as Tommy shouted, "It's Joe Namath!"

"C'mon, guys you know nobody can beat Dan Marino!" said another guy at the bar.

"Hey, let's not forget Johnny Unitas!" Billy had to throw in his two cents.

A dining patron called into the bar, "Sorry fellas, but you forgot Terry Bradshaw."

Dennis leaned on the bar to have a private chat with Matt while avoiding the hoopla from the rest of the men.

"How's the work coming along?" he asked.

"We're working ten to twelve hour shifts some days."

"That sounds grueling," remarked Dennis.

"It's not the hours that are grueling; it's the trudging through mud and muck while maneuvering massive coils of electrical wire that's brutal. We're trying to restore power to residents whose power stations have been stabilized," he explained. "Most of the out-of-towners are willing to work the hours so we can finish up and go home. Some nights I'm too tired and dirty to do anything but go home, shower, and get into bed."

"Julie doesn't seem to mind," Dennis commented.

Matt and Julie looked at each other and decided to call it a night. They were both tired and had to work the next day. No one took note of their leaving except for Dennis since the others were still embroiled in their quarterback debate.

Once home Matt went right upstairs while Julie quickly tidied up. It had been a long tedious day for both of them. She was disappointed to find Matt fast asleep when she got into bed. She thought he was so thoughtful to leave his lamp on for her. She was still shaken up over the dispute between the two young customers earlier that evening and wanted to hear Matt's opinion, but most of all she missed his good-night kiss.

SUNDAY, OCTOBER 9

Julie snuggled naked in Matt's arms as they read the morning paper together, basking in the afterglow of their earlier lovemaking. Her peace was interrupted by a call from her mother in Florida. She knew right away that David had told her mother about Matt. Her mother, although extremely hurt and disappointed, had forgiven David for his infidelity and maintained a close relationship with him despite his and Julie's divorce. Her mom had moved to a condo beach community just outside Naples ten years ago after the death of Julie's father. Despite the loss, after some time, her mother was able to make many new friends and become socially independent, relieving Julie of any responsibility. However, they kept in constant contact and visited each other frequently. In fact, in all her excitement, Julie had temporarily forgotten about her two-week Florida visit planned for the end of the month. It would have to be postponed indefinitely; she knew her mother would be disappointed, but she would find a way to make it up to her at a later time.

"Hello, Mother," she said. "I really don't want to discuss this with you right now. Yes, what David told you is true, but like I said, not now. We can talk about it another time." She cringed as she said the words, "I'm going to be changing my reservation for the end of the month. I don't know when. Please trust me on this. I'll be sure to call you soon and give you all the details. I promise I'll let you know, but I have to go now," she said to delay the inevitable lecture and added "I love you," as she quickly hung up.

She wanted to wring David's neck, she thought, but not right now as she rolled back over toward Matt and resumed their cuddle.

"Is everything all right?" he asked.

"Everything is fine," she assured him as she began to suck his nipple in an attempt to arouse him. He dropped the newspaper onto the floor and took her into his arms for another romp before they started out on their day trip.

It was a perfect fall day for their outing to Mystic Seaport. The foliage was spectacular with colors so vibrant that not even postcards could have captured the beauty. Julie chose a scenic route that would take over an hour through the rural areas of Connecticut. It was amazing to actually see that the storm had not affected many of these places. They decided to stop at a country inn for breakfast. It was a small cabin-like structure set back from the road. The smell of bacon and fresh coffee permeated the dining room as they walked into the inn. They were seated in a breakfast-type nook set off from the rest of the room. Julie couldn't help thinking to herself that she and Matt must have the word *lovers* stamped on their foreheads. They sat next to each other in the same booth as they fed each other breakfast and played footsie under the table.

Like, two young lovers, they walked hand in hand while taking in the beauty of nature. The air was crisp and the sky a clear blue. Julie hoped the peace she felt was an omen of a happy and blissful future. Matt told Julie how he loved to go hiking this time of year with a friend up and down the Palisades along the Hudson River. The foliage there, too, he told her, was magnificent this time of year. He described the high jagged cliffs overlooking the Hudson with a view of the Statue of Liberty to the Tappan Zee Bridge. He didn't mention, however, that the friend he was referring to was Katie.

"This was always my favorite time of year," Matt said. "Probably because it's so temporary and I never have time to weary of it."

The closer they got to the seaport, the more excited Matt became. When he saw the old whaling ship the *Charles W. Morgan,* he was in awe.

"Wow, is she beautiful!" he said, gaping at the massive ship. He started running to the ship making it hard for Julie to keep up with him, and she marveled at Matt's child-like delight. Once aboard, he stood at the helm as though he were the captain shouting orders to anyone that would listen.

"Ahoy, mate! Port out! Starboard home! Prepare to disembark!" She didn't know whether she should be embarrassed or not. He was having so much fun being a big kid, and she didn't want to ruin it for him; after all, he had confided in her how he been cheated out of this experience years ago. Little did she know, Matt actually had no good childhood memories!

They decided to take the horse-and-carriage ride around the re-created nineteenth-century village so they could fully experience first-hand the feeling of the period. Many of the buildings were originals that were transported from different places in New England. They visited the old shipyard and watched the workers plying the trades of the times—the ship smiths, coopers, woodcarvers, and riggers. Matt took a turn at participating in re-enacting each of the trades only to find that he was more confused about what he wanted to be when he grew up. Julie had to constantly bring him back to reality with passionate kisses. They had a picture taken together wearing clothes of the era, and Julie felt like she had traveled back on a time machine. The thought of churning butter or hand washing the family's laundry, however, repulsed her as she imagined the calloused hands she would have instead of her own baby soft ones. In contrast, Matt didn't want to take off his seadog outfit and insisted that he might just board any seafaring vessel passing through and head for parts unknown.

Julie and Matt visited the Mystic Seaport Lighthouse that stood at the westernmost point of the seaport and was as nostalgic as the village itself. The salty breeze from the sea was both relaxing and exhilarating making them feel completely refreshed. The film exhibit of the lighthouses in the United States included some along the Jersey shore, and Matt found himself thinking of Katie, Ann Marie, and the girls. Julie snapped him out of his trance when she nudged him to show him the many seagulls flying above in a breathtaking formation.

Julie had more fun than she had had in a long time. The best part of her day was when Matt pulled her into a secluded brush area and made love to her. She had never done anything as sexually daring as this, taking a chance of being observed. He took her to levels of ecstasy she had never reached before. Their ride home was peaceful, and although they were both tired, they were exhilarated from the events of their day. She fell asleep in his arms totally convinced that he was her destiny.

MONDAY, OCTOBER 10

The next morning, Matt was still talking about their trip and how he had always wanted to be a sailor. He had planned on joining the Navy right out of high school, but his financial obligations to his sickly mother had squelched that dream. He remembered how he had continued to support her until she died. Maybe, if not for his mother, he and Katie would already own a house. Julie interrupted his reverie to remind him that Jack was coming for him.

"It's time for you to ship out, mate," she jested.

"Aye, aye, captain," he laughed as he kissed her and ran for the door.

Seconds later he was talking to his wife. "Hi, Katie."

"Hi love," she answered with a yawn.

"I'm sorry to wake you again, but it really is the only time I know I have cell reception."

"It's okay; I need to get up anyway. I must have overslept today. It's the shore air I guess. Ann Marie and I took Laura and Suzie to the movies last night. How was your weekend?"

"I worked Saturday, but yesterday I went with one of the guys to Mystic Seaport," he said without thinking.

"Excuse me, but I thought you said you were working all weekend.

"We were blessed with an afternoon dismissal." The lie rolled off his tongue.

"If we had known sooner, Laura and I could have driven up and gone with you," she sighed.

"Unfortunately, it was last minute because Jack wasn't feeling well. But anyway I got to play captain! What do you think of that?'

"You are such a big kid, but I'm glad you had a chance to relax and have fun.'"

"I really would like to come back with Laura one day,"

"I'm sure she would like that," Katie responded.

"Oh, by the way, did you remember to get bowling subs for us?" "Yes, I took care of it. Ann Marie got a couple she knows to fill in."

"That's good. But I still don't see why you can't bowl without me."

"I wouldn't feel right leaving Laura with someone while you're away. Besides, I would feel so guilty bowling without my better half," she said with a sigh.

"Here comes Jack: I gotta go! I love you, Kates, and don't forget to give my baby girl a kiss for me," he said as he quickly hung up and continued to wait for his ride.

Julie had a lot to do before she went to work the lunch shift at the Sahara. David called and insisted on dropping by to discuss buying the house. She agreed to his visit as long as he didn't interfere with her personal life, meaning Matt. She answered the door to find him standing with a rose in his teeth, which defused her intent to reprimand him for calling her mother. Although she often found his interference aggravating, there were times that he warmed her heart, and this was one of them. She had to give him credit for his determination, annoying as it could be, but as she told him many times before, he could be investing in a new relationship instead of wasting his time on her.

"Come on in," she said, as he handed her the rose.

"A beautiful rose for a beautiful woman," he said.

"I really don't have much time, so please tell me what you have on your mind," she insisted.

"Julie, I have a proposal for you, and I want you to hear me out. I'm willing to buy this house if you do decide to move. But because of the uncertain circumstances, I don't want to take advantage of you, so I'll take over total financial responsibility for the house until you're absolutely sure that you won't be coming back, and only then will I buy the house from you. This house means a lot to me, and I couldn't bear to have strangers living here," he said.

"That seems fair enough, but I'm sure once I move I won't be coming back."

"Well, can we hug and kiss on the deal?" he asked. She smiled at him as she reached out and embraced him, and they kissed each other on the cheek.

"By the way, please keep this just between the two of us for the time being," she pleaded.

"Of course," he agreed. David had no doubt in his mind that this deal would never come to fruition and that Julie would remain there given his suspicions about Matt. He hoped and prayed for the day that he would have Julie back in his arms for good, and he promised himself that he would never let her go.

That evening Matt made his way to Conor's to watch the Monday night football game with the guys while Julie worked. Everyone was glad to see Matt, and he enjoyed the locals that hung out there, but he was surprised to find that none of the women were present except for Allie, the barmaid. She knew that her place during the game was to keep quiet and to keep the drinks flying. The guys told Matt that women were only allowed on Sundays while they watched the game as long as they weren't a nuisance, but Monday night during football season was strictly stag night at Conor's. It amused Matt that everyone had accepted this ritual, and it seemed to be the law of the land or the neighborhood, for that matter. The women insisted that the men make it up to them after football season. He took his seat next to Chris as the pregame show began.

Bobby called over to Matt, "I hear a lot of people are still without service. How long do you think it will be before everything is back to normal?"

Matt answered back, "I have no clue. There is still a lot of water keeping us from getting to downed wires. In some areas, we're rebuilding the power plants."

"I bet Julie hopes it never gets fixed so you never have to leave," said Chris.

Matt just said, "I'll stay as long as I need to," then he called Allie over for another drink. Chris, however, interpreted Matt's response optimistically: so when Matt went to the men's room, he told everyone he was sure Matt intended to continue his relationship with Julie after his work was done in Connecticut.

Luckily for Matt, it was time for kick-off when he got back to the bar. Matt threw his arms up in the air like a goal post and shouted to his fellow bar seat referees, "Let the hooting and hollering begin." Arguments continued throughout the game. How ten men could watch the same game and interpret it differently was beyond Allie. Hers was not to question why, though—hers was but to keep their drinks coming or die. She was also responsible for setting up the football pool each week, which she really didn't mind since the winner always gave her a percentage.

The petty arguments amused Allie. She could care less who was a better quarterback, Mark Sanchez or Eli Manning since she wouldn't recognize either of them if they stood in front of her. Allie was simply glad that they and their teammates kept the patrons entertained for a couple of hours, which made her job a bit easier. She kept her eyes open for that almost empty glass to fill, which happened at a pretty frequent pace during these Monday night games.

The game lasted just over three hours with the Giants victorious over the Jets. Julie had arrived at the end of the game to find that Matt had won the pool and was buying drinks for the gang. She decided to stay for a drink and share in the fun with the guys. She added to Matt's excitement when she told him that not only did her bowling league agree to let Matt sub, but also he would be the second sub on the same team as her. It turned out that the honeymooners who needed subs were a couple on the same bowling team. Matt was delighted when she told him the news. He became animated and took the pose of a bowler with a ball in his hand and extended his arm out as though he were rolling the ball out to meet the imaginary pins.

"I think that was a strike," Bobby called from across the bar.

"Well, it was a perfect stance anyway," added Chris. They all broke into laughter at the sight.

Julie took home a very happy Giants fan, and Matt couldn't wait until he saw Tommy the next day to rub it in. But for now, he was interested in getting home and trying to impress Julie with some special football moves in bed. With a little simulation and training, he hoped she'd become more interested in the actual sport.

TUESDAY, OCTOBER 11, AND EARLY WEDNESDAY, OCTOBER 12

'Where does he get his energy?' thought Julie to herself as Matt somersaulted out of bed. He was like the Energizer bunny that never quits. She was ten paces behind him as they went down for breakfast. He only wanted coffee this morning, since he and Jack planned to stop at the local bagel store. She wasn't working until later so she thought she might just go back to bed for a while.

This morning Matt was pacing back and forth faster than usual, thought Julie, as she watched him from the window. It was becoming a morning ritual for him. Who could he be talking to this early in the morning? She was comfortable assuming it was probably Jack or Kevin and was determined not to pry; after all, it was none of her business, and he was certainly entitled to his privacy. Regardless, she was determined to be vigilant. *'Could David's concerns about Matt have*

any possible validity?' she wondered. *'How could she even give thought to that knowing how jealous David was?'*

Matt was actually concerned that Katie had not answered any of his three calls. He could have sworn she and the girls were coming home from the shore last night. Maybe they had stayed another night. They could even have spent the night at Ann Marie's house or with Katie's mother, but he couldn't remember her mentioning that she had any plans. He would try her again later when he got a chance. He was glad to see Jack driving up the street toward him.

"Good morning, boss," he said as he got into the car.

"Good morning to you. How did you like the game last night? Did you see those Giants run all over the Jets?"

"That's two losses two weeks in a row. It's not a good way to start a season. Poor Tommy will be singing the blues today."

"Where did you watch the game, at Julie's or at the bar?" asked Jack.

"At Conor's," he answered. "I am now officially a member of the Monday Night Bar Stool Quarterbacks. I really like the guys. They're a lot of laughs. You should have seen their reactions when Sanchez fumbled and Tuck ran the ball back thirty yards for the touchdown and the win. They were still whining and bellowing twenty minutes after the game ended. I love to watch grown men cry like babies."

"I think you just described Tommy," quipped Jack.

Later that day Matt answered his cell phone while splicing wires in the bucket; Tommy, wearing his earphones, sat in the truck and ate his lunch.

"Matt, it's Katie," but before she could say another word, he began berating her. "Where are you? I called the house three times this morning and you didn't answer."

"That's because I've been at the hospital with Laura all night, but before you start panicking, everything is all right, so calm down."

"Why? What happened? Is she all right?"

"She is fine," Katie answered and continued to explain. "She was crying that she had pains near her stomach, and she had a fever that wouldn't break. I got scared when I felt the heat coming from her abdomen so I took her to the emergency room. She had an emergency appendectomy this morning."

"She had it already and you didn't call me?" he shouted.

"Would you stop panicking? The doctor told me it was routine and that they could try a non-invasive procedure to remove her appendix using laparoscopic surgery. I didn't want you stuck up there consumed with worry while all this was going on. Of course, she is asking for you. She says she only wants her daddy, but I reassured her you would call and talk to her."

"Listen, I am going to try to borrow a car and get there as fast as I can."

"I really don't think it's necessary, Matt, a phone call will do."

Matt just ignored her and asked, "Where did you take her, Palisade General?"

"No, I took her to St. Mary's."

"Okay, just tell my little girl I'll be there as soon as I can and that I love her very much." With that, he hung up without even saying good-bye.

Matt immediately called Julie and asked to borrow her car overnight to go home for a family emergency. At first, she insisted on calling in sick to work and going with him, but he convinced her that he would feel awkward trying to make her feel comfortable while tending to the situation at hand. She assumed he didn't want her to meet his family under difficult circumstances. She met him and he dropped her at work before leaving for Jersey. Afterward, she realized he never mentioned what the emergency was. Dennis, her hero, agreed to drive her home from work later.

The trek down I-95 was the longest ride of his life. He couldn't think of anything but his little girl's arms wrapped around his neck while she bombarded him with her playful kisses. His eyes teared up thinking about how much he loved his little princess.

When Laura saw Matt walk into her hospital room, her eyes lit up, and despite being medicated, she tried to reach for Matt as he approached her.

"Oh, Daddy, I knew you would come. See, Mommy, now I feel better." Katie smiled at the two of them as Matt managed to lie on the bed next to Laura, who put her head on his chest. He kissed her head and stroked her hair. He blew a kiss to Katie who sat in a chair beside the bed, and she blew one back.

"How long are they keeping her?" he whispered since Laura was already sleeping on his chest.

"Only until tomorrow morning," she said.

"Why don't you go home, and I'll stay with her for the night. You must be exhausted after being here all last night and today. Honey, go get some sleep and come back around four so I can get back in time for work."

"I guess you're right." She leaned over and kissed him gently on the lips. "I am so glad that you decided to come home, Matt."

He looked at her and said, "I would never leave my two girls when they needed me."

Laura slept all through the night on Matt's chest but awoke when he tried to slither from underneath her, preparing to leave as soon as Katie returned.

"You make the best pillow, Daddy," she said, still drowsy. He just hugged her tightly. She knew exactly what to say to warm his heart. He had to get back to Connecticut in time for Jack to pick him up outside Julie's. He explained to Laura that he was leaving to go back to work as soon as Katie got there, but he would be home in just over a week and would try to call her every day.

"I'm going to ask Mommy if we can have a coming home party for you, Daddy!"

"Well, I can see you both had a great pajama party last night without me," Katie said upon entering the room as she pretended to pout. Laura giggled as she hugged Matt tighter.

"I guess Mommy just crashed our pajama party, princess," Matt said as he rose from her bed. Laura was quick to tell Katie about Matt's coming home party that they were going to have to plan. After lots of hugs and kisses for his girls, Matt left for Connecticut.

Julie was already up and about when Matt walked in. He stopped to give her a big hug and kiss as he ran off to get ready for Jack who would be there in fifteen minutes.

"Is everything okay?" she asked him through the bathroom door. He shouted back,

"Everything is fine, thank God. Thanks for lending me your car; you are a lifesaver."

"I'm glad I could help. Maybe we should call off bowling for tonight."

"Why? I'm looking forward to it." With that, he opened the door, kissed her cheek as he pushed past her, and shouted back, "I'll see you tonight." Then he rushed for the front door.

❊⚬❊

Matt wanted to be sure Laura was okay and was glad when he heard her little voice in the background when Katie answered her cell phone.

"Can I just say hello to her a sec?" he asked Katie. "Hi baby girl, how are you feeling?"

"Hi Daddy, Mommy is taking me home this morning," she answered. "I can't wait to see Suzie. Mommy said she can come over to visit me later."

"I'm glad you are feeling okay, but you have to take it easy, and you can't run around."

"I *know*, Daddy; Mommy gave me a lecture already," she sighed.

"Okay, let me talk to Mommy," he said as he blew kisses into the phone and she blew them back. "I'll try to call you later, but if I can't, then definitely tomorrow," he said as he watched Jack's car pull up.

WEDNESDAY NIGHT, OCTOBER 12

Julie was cleaning up after a busy lunch at the Sahara when she braced herself for a debilitating cramp in her abdomen. Dennis witnessed her wincing as she stood doubled over.

"Julie, what's wrong?" he asked as he helped her to a chair.

"I'm okay, Dennis. It's what you call getting used to frequent intimate relations."

"Are you trying to make me jealous?"

"No," she laughed. "I haven't been with anyone for over five years. My body had gotten used to the famine and is trying to adjust to the feasting now. I have to make a doctor's appointment for next week."

"I'm glad you're going to do that," he said, reassured.

Julie confided a lot in Dennis. He was a great listener and sounding board and was very gentle when he presented any objections or opinions. He knew what she went through with

David and the divorce and was always there for her. She told him how annoying David had become since she had gotten involved with Matt.

"Believe me," Dennis said, "he has beaten himself up over and over again for hurting you. Losing you devastated him even though he knew he deserved it. Cut him a little slack; he really is a good guy!"

"You're right. I'll try," she said.

Dennis was worried about Julie, and he never wanted anything bad to happen to her. He hoped Julie was right about her self-diagnosis, and it was nothing more. He knew that her problem probably couldn't be attributed to a pregnancy, unfortunately, since she and David had tried for years to have a baby and were told it was useless. Dennis remembered their sorrow at that time. In fact, it was the saddest he had ever seen Julie—worse than even the period leading up to and including her divorce.

The lanes thundered with the noise of bowling balls as Matt and Julie entered Betty's Bowling Alley. Immediately, Julie was called over to lane twelve by Carol and Vinnie, the Ten Pins, their bowling partners for the night. They were delighted that Julie was their sub tonight not only because of her high average but also because she was so much fun. She was the league's favorite sub. She introduced Matt to everyone when the opposing team, the Dead Ringers, arrived. His charisma never ceased to amaze her as people took to him so naturally. By the end of the night, the two teams were play-fully feuding friends.

Carol and Vinnie were a married couple who considered their Wednesday bowling to be their weekly date night. It was their way of sharing time and a mutual passion for bowling together. Vinnie was always quick with the witty remarks, but Matt had great comebacks for him. Their humor made the night enjoyable for all around them. The chemistry of the team was apparent in their scores as the rest of the league looked on with envy.

Despite their loss to the Ten Pins, the Dead Ringers enjoyed the good-natured chiding of their opponents. Their three games ended much earlier than the other teams because the Ten Pins rolled so many strikes and eliminated the second ball for a pickup of the remaining pins. Matt impressed everyone with his unique curve ball that headed for the gutter and then took a surprise turn at the very last second.

"I've been bowling for years, Matt, and have never seen a curveball like yours," said Vinnie. "Do you think we could meet up one day for practice, and you could teach me your technique?"

"Anytime," answered Matt.

Both teams decided to end their night at the bar with a drink before going home. After they had their drinks in front of them, Kimberly from the Dead Ringers toasted, "To the victors belong the spoils," as she instructed the bartender to give the check to the winners.

Matt responded, "That's the least we can do after steam-rolling you guys tonight," as he paid the tab for the drinks. Everyone was astonished to learn that Julie and Matt had just met. They were under the impression the two had been together for some time based on their natural interactions. Matt was extremely demonstrative with Julie in public, giving her little hugs and kisses and constantly stroking her hair. They seemed like the perfect couple.

THURSDAY, OCTOBER 13

What a beautiful morning this is, Julie thought, as she lay sprawled naked on her bed. She had woken up to Matt nibbling on her breast which sent tingling sensations throughout her entire body. She wished she could wake up to such energizing morning sex every day. He even brought her a cup of coffee in bed and insisted that she stay there. Thankfully, her cramping ceased in bed and seemed to occur only when she was on her feet for any length of time.

Matt had been with her now over a week, yet her life was turned upside down. She was head over heels in love with him but didn't want to scare him away by verbally expressing her emotions. She had asked him to stay with her temporarily to help him out, not expecting to become so personally involved. She was going to enjoy him for as long as it lasted, but she was sure that if their relationship continued this way, he would become her permanent lodger.

At the same time, Julie wanted to keep herself grounded. She didn't want to face another devastating loss or disappointment as she did with David after she caught him with that other woman. The experience had reduced her to a shell, void and empty with no feelings. Julie wanted so badly to regain some passion in her life. Matt had accomplished this for her. Now she had so much passion she felt she just might explode.

If only she could lie like this in wait for him to come home, spring her animal desires on him, and continue where they left off this morning, but no, she had things to do today. She had a lunch date with Nancy, a girlfriend from high school. They got together every few months to catch up on the events in their lives. Julie never had much news to share with Nancy. Her life was more or less status quo until now. She was dying to tell Nancy about Matt, her perfect gentleman.

She quickly got up and showered while she made a mental list of her duties for the day. She wasn't working so the whole day belonged to her. After lunch, she planned on picking up the sports paraphernalia for tomorrow's game. Matt had suggested dinner out tonight and maybe a drink or two at Conor's. She decided to surprise him with some nice attire, knowing he only brought casual and work things with him. She couldn't remember the last time that her social calendar had been so full. In fact, she never needed a calendar at all, since her basic schedule was work. She worked any and all shifts that were offered to her at the Sahara. She needed to stay busy to fill the empty days of not having a relationship. Her life was so much better now that Matt had filled that void.

Julie found Nancy sitting at a table waiting for her as she scurried into Heather's Local Luncheonette. After a friendly kiss on the cheek, Nancy squinted suspiciously at Julie and remarked,

"There's something different about you, Julie. What is it?"

Julie beamed as she blurted out, "I'm in love with the most handsome and greatest guy in the world!"

"*Really*, and where did you meet this Mr. Wonderful?" Nancy asked.

"At the Sahara," exclaimed Julie. "Would you believe it? He just walked into my life."

Julie gave Nancy all the details of the last week.

Nancy, being a skeptic, asked, "What else do you know about this guy other than he's good looking and great in bed?"

"He's single, has a good job, and is extremely charismatic. He fits in wherever he goes. He's just amazing," she replied.

"I'm glad to see you happy again, but, honey, please take it slow," Nancy begged. "He's not here forever. It's probably only temporary."

"I really believe we will work out our distance problem. One of us will move if we have to," Julie stated.

"I can't believe you let your guard down so easily and let yourself to be taken in by this guy. Now, please promise me that you will stay sensible, and you won't make any rash decisions about this Romeo without seeking some objective advice. What does David say about this?" she asked.

"He thinks I'm crazy, and it's not a good idea, but then David can't be objective when it comes to me, no matter how hard he tries," Julie explained.

"I believe he loves you very much and always has your best interests at heart," Nancy replied.

"Well, I don't know about that, but I do know that I have to get going. I have a list of things to do before Matt gets home. We'll have to get together again soon, Nancy. I always enjoy seeing you," Julie said.

"Believe me, I'll be keeping in touch," Nancy replied. After a big hug and kiss, Julie was on the run again. She was so light-hearted that she felt like a feather in the wind.

Julie found exactly what she wanted for the game at the local sports store. She bought a jersey for each of them with matching baseball caps—Yankees for Matt and, of course, Red Sox for herself. To complete their ensembles, she purchased team throws to wrap around them since it was a fall night and they were going to the game in an outdoor stadium. She quickly stopped at Ian's Menswear before having her nails done; then headed home to set the stage for this morning's encore.

After showering and primping for this evening's conquest, Julie lay naked upon her queen-sized bed. She had replaced her cotton sheets with deep red satin ones she had bought that afternoon. She could hardly suppress her excitement as she lay in wait for Matt. It wasn't long until she heard him come in and call out for her.

"Up here, honey!" she shouted back to him. She could hear him taking two steps at a time up the stairs.

"What are you doing up here?" he said upon entering the room. "Ooh," he moaned when he caught sight of her. His clothes were off in seconds, and he became the one in attack mode as he pounced onto the bed and began groping and sucking her from head to toe. He pleasured her into an orgasm before she reciprocated, and just before he reached his climax, she straddled him as they both rode into sexual exhilaration.

"Oh, honey, I just can't get enough of you," he panted as he laid spread on the bed.

"You can have me anytime you want," she murmured as she cuddled into him with a content smile, and they both slipped into a brief nap. She awoke to find Matt in the shower where she joined him for a quick rinse.

They were seated at a table for two next to a window with a view of the star-studded sky. It was so romantic in this formal dining room at Jacques Restaurant. The crystal chandeliers complimented the ivory cameo wallpaper and the dark mauve and wine-colored Aubusson carpet flecked with gold.

Matt wore the new clothes that Julie had surprised him with earlier: an ecru dress shirt set against a dark brown suit jacket and a small diamond patterned tie of the same colors outlined in black. Julie thought he was the most handsome gentleman in the restaurant. She had decided to wear a classic black sleeveless fitted dress that she accented with a string of pearls and matching teardrop pearl earrings. They were totally enamored with each other, as Matt tried to slip off her open-toed high-heeled sandal under the table.

"Do you think you'll feel up to a triple header tonight when we get home?" she asked.

"I'm always up for you," he said. "You can feel for yourself," he quipped, as his eyes sparkled with mischief.

"I know how hard you can be," she teased back in a whisper.

They toasted each other as they sipped their champagne and perused the menu. They decided to share chateaubriand and settled into enjoying each other's company after they placed their order.

"How do you like living up here?" she asked as nonchalantly as possible.

"It's a slower pace than what I'm used to, coming from the New York area, and I really don't think I could live up here," he answered honestly. He was sure she understood his temporary status since she was the one who stated it when they met, and he didn't want to embarrass her by emphasizing it.

Her heart sank for a second, before she thought, Oh well, I guess I'm moving. Her thoughts continued to race, we could have a long-distance relationship until I sold or rented the house and got things in order. David would help me when the time came and he knew we were serious. She began to smile at Matt while she thought about their future arrangements. She would wait until he broached the subject; she just wanted to be ready.

'Oohs' and 'aahs' greeted the enchanted couple when they entered Conor's following their meal.

"You two look spectacular. I wish I had my camera," cried Anna.

"What affair are you two coming from?" asked Chris.

"We had dinner at Jacques," replied Julie.

As Allie presented them with their drinks, she announced, "Your drinks are on the house since we haven't ever been graced by such royalty."

The group all responded in unison with, "Here, here" as they raised their glasses in a toast.

"This is a wedding that I want to be invited to," declared Bobby.

"Let's not get ahead of ourselves," snapped Matt as he walked away from the bar with his drink.

Everyone glared at Bobby to indicate he had said something stupid, but Julie quickly added, "We've only just met. Give us a chance." Bobby offered a silent apology to Julie, and she nodded back in acceptance knowing his remark was innocent and meant no harm. The incident left everyone with the impression that Matt was trying to deal with their possible long-distance dilemma without any outside interference. After different conversations began again at the bar, Matt made his way back to accept another drink bought for him before asking Julie if she minded if they left soon since they had a big night ahead of them tomorrow. After they bid their good nights, they rode home in silence. Since Julie assumed Matt was struggling with decisions about their future, she was determined not to address it herself and would do her best to deter anyone else from doing so.

Once at home, Matt kissed Julie's lips slightly and then feigned exhaustion. That left her to rue Bobby's premature comment that had ended their almost perfect night. She knew there would be no triple play tonight. She would have to hope for that tomorrow night at Fenway Park.

FRIDAY, OCTOBER 14

Julie awoke to find Matt bouncing around her bedroom. He had placed pillows and objects on the floor to use as bases and swung a backscratcher as an imaginary bat.

"Are you going to watch the game tonight or are you playing in it?" she quipped, as he jumped on the bed and wrestled her playfully. He then gave her a quick kiss and headed for the shower as she went down to prepare his breakfast.

"Remember, we have to leave by three thirty because it's about a two-and-a-half-hour drive to Boston," Julie reminded him.

"I thought we were taking the train," he said.

"We'd never make it in time," she answered. She explained that she had checked and found that it was a twenty-minute drive to the nearest Amtrak train station in Berlin where they would have to catch a train to New Haven; then they would have to switch trains to Boston's Back Bay station, which was about two miles from Fenway. Taking everything into consideration, they would be lucky if they made it by eight o'clock.

He agreed driving would guarantee their arrival at Fenway on time. He wanted to be settled and comfortable for the first pitch just after seven o'clock.

"Okay, I'll have Jack drop me off by three thirty so we can run," he said.

"And I have another waitress coming in early to relieve me, so I should be home by then, too," she replied. She walked him to the door to ensure her good-bye kiss.

When Julie looked out the window, she saw him jumping in the air with his hands extending up, as though he were practicing catching a fly ball. She wasn't sure if she was going to the game with a man or a boy. She laughed at the thought as she saw the cell phone come out and the pacing begins. She had her own business to attend to before she left for work.

"Hi babe," Matt said as Katie answered the phone. "How are my girls?"

"We're fine, honey."

"How is Laura feeling?" he asked.

"She's back to her usual self, so you don't have to worry," Katie assured him. "You can see for yourself this weekend." Before Matt could respond Katie added, "By the way, were you by any chance using our credit card last night about nine o'clock?"

"Yes, I took one of the guys out to dinner," he answered. "Why are you asking?"

"I was ordering a Halloween costume online for Laura and my card was rejected; when I called Visa, they said someone was using it in Connecticut. I explained that you were up there on business and they tried to call you and confirm it but I guess you were in a no cell service area. They'll probably try to reach you today to verify what I've already told them. Can you keep an eye on your phone, or even better, maybe call them? I really want to get this costume for Laura before it sells out," she explained.

"Sure, honey, I can do that.

"She is so excited about seeing you this weekend. So am I of course!

"Oh about this weekend- it is still up in the air. Jack hasn't said if we're working or not. Look, I have to go. Jack is pulling up! Take care of yourself and my baby girl," he said quickly as he blew two kisses into the phone before hanging up. He could hear her voice beginning to rise just as he pushed the end button on his phone.

"Good morning, Jack," said Matt as he got into the car.

"Hi Matt," he answered. "Could you do me a favor, and not mention anything today to the other guys about me letting you knock off work early for the game? I don't want to hear them complaining about working twelve-hour days and you leaving again, especially after you left early on Tuesday," Jack explained. "Billy and Tommy are okay with it, but I really don't want to hear it from the others."

"Of course I won't mention it. You know that I sincerely appreciate you letting me take the time off," said Matt.

"Have you ever been to Fenway?" asked Jack.

"Nope. In fact, I've never even been to Boston," he replied.

"You are in for a real treat," Jack said. "There's nothing like being there in person and seeing the Green Monster."

"It looks impressive on TV," Matt agreed.

"I'm sure you and Julie will have a wonderful time," Jack said.

"I plan on it," Matt replied.

Julie had a busy lunch rush and was running around from table to table when she noticed Mr. and Mrs. Reynolds standing by the door waiting to be seated. She greeted them both with a big hug and thanked them for the tickets to tonight's game as she showed them to their table. They were delighted to see Julie so happy for the first time in a long while. They were very fond of her, mainly because she always took a personal interest in them when they ate at the Sahara.

"I hope you enjoy the seats tonight," Mr. Reynolds said. "I wanted to let you know the section that you're sitting in includes waiter service, so you don't even have to get up," he told her. "Won't it be nice for a change for you to be the one getting served at your seat?"

"You're kidding! I am just so excited," she said, as she quickly went to get their drinks and check on her other customers. Mr. and Mrs. Reynolds weren't happy when they found out that she picked up their lunch tab, but Julie insisted she needed to show her appreciation for their kindness.

"I'll be watching for you on TV tonight," said Mr. Reynolds as he got up to leave.

Julie and Matt met back at the house at about the same time and immediately changed into their game jerseys and jeans and ran out the door. They were actually on the road before three thirty to avoid the Friday evening traffic in and around Boston as much as possible. Julie had researched different routes to Fenway and was able to cut the travel time considerably by driving eighty miles an hour, while Matt took in as much scenery as he could; given the speed they were traveling. Julie tried to avoid as many traffic snarls as possible; at the same time, she wanted Matt to see something of Boston while they were there.

She drove around Boston Common and along Beacon Street to show Matt the building that was used for the old TV sitcom *Cheers.*

"You mean to tell me the show itself wasn't filmed there?" Matt asked in disbelief.

"That's right; the inside looks totally different than the TV show, which was filmed in a movie studio in front of a live audience," Julie explained. "Believe me, I think everyone is disappointed when they realize this," she said. "I know I was." They continued on to Quincy Market where she parked while Matt made a mad dash inside to see what it was like. He quickly bought a heart necklace for Laura that he couldn't resist. He had the salesman put it in a tiny gift bag instead of a box, so he could stuff it in his pocket and then he ran back out to Julie. They rode along the Charles River so Matt could look across at the prestigious MIT as they passed Boston University.

"I really never knew there was so much to see up here," he said in wonderment.

"There is also a Freedom Trail that you can follow that allows you to walk to all the different Revolutionary sites in and around Boston." Julie told Matt. "It's too bad we don't have enough time for Boston Harbor tonight." The thought of Matt dressed as Indian throwing boxes of tea into the harbor amused her. She was sure he would be the first person to volunteer to participate in the re-enactment of the Boston Tea Party.

"We'll have to leave that for another time," she quickly added, as they drove toward Fenway Park ahead on their left.

"Wow, I can't believe I'm here," Matt said in amazement.

Once inside, the magic started. They were ushered to their special field box seats, as though they were celebrities. Julie forgot that Matt was wearing Yankee garb until she saw some of the Red Sox fans' sneers. She laughed to herself thinking of how they must look, both of them fans of the rival teams. Their seats were incredibly situated between third base and home plate with the imposing thirty-six-plus-foot Green Monster to their left. Matt was so in awe that Julie couldn't get a word out of him, and yet she noticed something odd about his demeanor.

"How can you see anything with your baseball cap pulled down like that?" she asked.

"It's the field lights that are blinding me," he said. He must have very sensitive eyes, she thought, since the lights weren't bothering her in the least.

"Mr. Reynolds said that he'll watch for us on TV, so be sure to try to catch the foul balls that come our way," she said. He was so busy reading his game program and looking around from under his cap that he wasn't even paying attention to her. Matt was much more subdued than Julie had expected he would be. He did more jumping around and cheering at home than here, she observed, and for a brief moment, she wondered why.

The game began as usual with the "Star Spangled Banner" sung beautifully by some famous singer unfamiliar to either Matt or Julie, but evidently well known to the crowd as they roared in approval. They were in the second row and so close they felt as though they could reach out and touch the players. Oddly, Matt showed no emotion even when Alex Rodriguez, his favorite Yankee, ran right past him toward home plate to score three times in the first few innings. Julie attributed it to the excitement although he seemed to distance himself as she roared and cheered for her team. She hoped that he wasn't getting sick.

They watched the game intensely, each with a hot dog in one hand and a beer in the other. The Yankees led the Red Sox five to nothing until the sixth inning and then the Sox took off. Kevin Youkilis, Boston's third baseman, belted a homer with three men on, bringing them within reach of New York. Julie couldn't stay in her seat as she jumped up cheering, while Matt slunk lower in his seat. She interpreted this as a reaction to the Red Sox scoring.

During the seventh inning stretch, they went to the Hall of Fame Club and looked at all the retired Red Sox players' memorabilia, especially Ted Williams and Wade Boggs.

"I never knew Babe Ruth started his career as a Red Sox pitcher," said Matt. "I'm so disillusioned after thinking all these years he was always a Yankee!"

"Ha! He belonged to us first," she said, although she was admittedly a bit surprised that Matt, who was such an avid baseball fan, didn't know this bit of common trivia. Julie was relieved to think that Matt was feeling better when he put his arm around her and gave her a smooch on the lips. When the game resumed and they returned to their seats, he reverted back to his earlier stoic mood.

Julie became too involved in the game after that to notice anything while the Sox whipped past the Yanks in the eighth, scoring three when David Ortiz ripped a home run into the seats enabling Dustin Pedroia and Jacoby Ellsbury to score. The stadium went wild, except for Matt, who seemed to sink a little deeper into his seat as the TV cameras scoped the crowd. In the top of the ninth the Yankees amazingly tied the game. Julie could not believe Matt had so little reaction to this exciting turn of events. However, the clincher came in the bottom of the ninth when Manny Ramirez fired one out of the park just past the Green Monster, driving in Youkalis and Ortiz. Fenway Park thundered with cheers while Matt received scornful looks from some of the home team fans.

The traffic was gruesome getting out of the ballpark and Boston for that matter, but once on the highway, Julie floored it, getting them home in less than three hours. Matt became his animated self on the drive home, narrating a minute-by-minute replay to Julie. She had to remind him that she was at the game with him and saw it for herself. She was a bit baffled at his delayed reaction to such an exciting game.

Once home and settled in bed, he pulled out a bag and gave it to Julie. She opened it to find a new Red Sox T-shirt.

"When did you buy this?" she asked in amazement.

"When you went to the ladies' room," he answered proudly. She reached over to kiss him as he gathered her into his arms and she whispered into his ear,

"Thank you." He was becoming more and more of an enigma to Julie as each day passed.

SATURDAY, OCTOBER 15

Julie was startled awake by a crashing noise coming from the kitchen. She quickly ran down, stood at the kitchen door, and watched Matt bending down, attempting to put every pot and pan back where they belonged in the cabinet. He was becoming more and more frustrated as they kept falling back onto the floor. Julie made her presence known with a loud chuckle and offered her assistance.

"Honey, you can't put a pan or pot on top of a lid; let me do this," she said. He gladly stepped aside and watched as she reorganized everything back into the proper place.

"There," she said as she stood back up.

"I planned on surprising you with breakfast this morning," he said.

"You certainly surprised me with your good intent, but let me worry about the breakfast while you take your shower," she offered.

"Thanks," he said as he kissed her and made a relieved dash out of the kitchen. He was back down the stairs before she knew it and was devouring the meal in front of him.

"Oops, Jack will be here any minute," he said as he jumped up from the table, gave Julie a kiss, and ran out the door.

"Hi honey," said Matt and suddenly remembering Katie's request from yesterday, he added, "Oh no, I'm sorry, but I forgot to call the credit card company."

"Not to worry, love, it's all been taken care of. They evidently believed me when I told them you were the one using the card in Connecticut," she said.

"Oh, thank goodness," he sighed in relief. "So you were able to order Laura's costume?"

"Yes, everything is fine, so stop worrying."

"I'm sorry, but I was so busy yesterday. By the way, Kates, I don't think I'll be home tomorrow."

"Again Matt! Do I have to drive up there to see what's going on? Laura will be so disappointed," she said, "and so am I. This was not what you originally promised!"

"I'll see what Jack says later," he said. "Speak of the devil, here he comes. I'll call you tomorrow," he said. Before she had a chance to answer, he blew her a kiss, said "I love you," and hung up.

"So how was the game?" Jack asked excitedly.

"You wouldn't believe it, Jack. The players were right there in front of us. I wanted to reach out and high-five A-Rod each time he ran past me to score. Oh, and you were right about the thrill of the Green Monster. *And* let's not forget that we were served in our seats," he blabbed on like an eager child.

"Did you get to see any of Boston?" Jack asked.

"Sure did," answered Matt. "My tour guide gave me a flash ride by Boston Commons and the *Cheers* bar. I even got the chance to run in to see Quincy Market," he boasted.

"Wow, what a tour you had!" laughed Jack.

"It's just too bad the Yanks lost," said Matt.

"I wasn't too happy about that either," Jack agreed.

"I didn't realize you were a Yankee fan," said Matt in surprise.

"Sure am; grew up in the Bronx. I didn't move up here until I was married. So you see, Matt, you never know where you might end up," he added as they reached the job site.

Julie heard the phone ringing just as she was coming out of the shower. She ran and answered it,

"Hello," she said.

"Hello, Julie, is that you?" her mother asked.

"Yes, Mother, of course, it's me," said Julie.

"I have been so worried about you and not hearing back after our last call. What is going on in your life?" she asked frantically.

"Don't worry; everything's fine. I couldn't be happier," she said. "I am standing here dripping wet since I just got out of the shower. I really can't talk now but when I get time, I promise I'll call and give you the run down."

"Julie, I think I may need to come up and see for myself what is happening with you," her mother threatened.

"Do as you like, but for now I need to go dry off and get ready for work. I'll be sure to call you within the next couple of days. I love you very much, Mother," she said as she quickly hung up.

Matt asked Jack to drop him off at the Sahara after work to wait for Julie. He was glad to get off early again Saturday after the tedious week but was sorry that Jack couldn't join him tonight because he had a family commitment. As Matt took the last available seat at the bar, he looked around for Julie. She snuck up behind him, planted a big smooch on his lips, and ran off quickly to drop a check at her last table.

When she returned after her shift work was finished, she found Matt and Dennis deep in conversation. Matt stood and insisted she take his seat as he continued talking. Matt was answering Dennis with,

"I grew up in Hoboken, New Jersey."

Dennis's face lit up as he asked, "Isn't that where they filmed the movie *On the Waterfront* with Marlon Brando?"

"Sure is," answered Matt.

Dennis, an avid movie buff, added, "What a classic. It's one of my favorites. I could watch that movie over and over and not get sick of it."

"Me too," replied Matt. "Did you know that *On the Waterfront* is the only movie in which the Italian liner, the Andrea Doria, was featured before it collided off Nantucket in 1956?"

"No, I didn't. That's something for me to read up on." said Dennis. Now totally engrossed, he asked, "Does Hoboken really look like the movie?"

"It did then," Matt answered. "The waterfront itself may have changed drastically, but the rest of the city looks the same for the most part. Most streets have old attached brownstones several stories high with no elevators. It still has traditional close-knit neighborhoods where people look out for each other, and neighbors still sit out on their open stoops and have their daily chats."

After Dennis had put another round of drinks in front of them, Matt asked Julie, "Would you mind dropping me at the train station in the morning? A cousin passed away, and I have to go to his wake tomorrow."

"I'm so sorry to hear about your cousin. Was it expected?" Julie asked.

"Yes, he had cancer," he said. "I checked and the train leaves at 8:00 a.m. and I can catch the last one back at night. I'm sorry to ask you to get up so early, knowing you will be working until late tomorrow night."

"Don't be silly, just take my car. I'll ask Dennis to pick me up on his way in tomorrow." Before Matt could say anything, Julie called Dennis over and asked him.

"Sure," he answered, "and I'll drop her off tomorrow night if you're not back before we close."

Matt said, "I really don't want to inconvenience anyone."

"No bother," said Dennis. "I'm sorry to hear about your cousin."

"Thank you," said Matt.

"Maybe we should get going since you've got to be up early tomorrow," suggested Julie.

"Sure," he said as he took her hand and helped her up from her seat, in his gentlemanly way.

"Good night, Dennis, and thanks for your help."

"My pleasure," said Dennis. "Just have a safe trip."

Once home the two prepared for bed. Matt was already lying down when Julie entered the room wearing a sexy periwinkle satin teddy that accented her auburn hair as well as her curvy body. Matt took one look at her and his temperature began to rise as well as did something else. She moved sensuously around the room as though she was unaware of his gaze. Her intentionally tantalizing movements intensified his lust. When she knew she had tortured him enough and had him salivating like one of Pavlov's dogs, she leaned over to give him a good night kiss. As he snatched her into the bed, he kissed her mouth and body fast and furiously. He couldn't wait any longer as he straddled her body on top of his and lifted her up and down slowly at first, then quicker and quicker until he shouted in euphoria.

After his sexual release, he panted, "What did you just do to me?"

She purred into his ear, "Just wanted to give you a little going away present. There'll be more when you get back." They fell asleep cuddled in each other's arms.

SUNDAY, OCTOBER 16

The ride home to Hoboken was a smooth one with no traffic. I might make it home in an hour and a half, thought Matt. He was relieved that Julie had loaned him her car since it saved him a lot of travel time. He really liked her and maybe if he wasn't married she could have been the one for him, he thought. He didn't like lying to her about his cousin, but he didn't want to complicate matters. Their temporary arrangement was working out just fine. He was thankful she wasn't a clingy possessive type of woman who was looking for some kind of commitment. He already had enough females in his life. He looked forward to spending an entire day with Katie and Laura and wanted to surprise them since he had told them he wasn't sure if he was going to make it home.

Julie took the opportunity to call her mother as she had promised. She thought it was a great time to do so while Matt was out of the house. She explained from the beginning until now how her relationship with Matt had progressed, as well as *her* future intentions. Her mother knew that Julie had been disillusioned with men because of David and hadn't dated since. She also knew that she had to handle this gently or Julie would totally reject her advice as she did David's.

"I am so happy for you, Julie. It's about time you found someone that cares about you," her mother lied. As far as she was concerned David was the only one for Julie and it was just a matter of time until Julie herself realized that. If David was right, and this guy was there in Connecticut only temporarily and had no intentions of continuing a relationship with Julie, she was in agreement with David that Julie would be devastated. On the other hand, if Julie was right and the fellow was honest and sincere, then she would have to accept Julie's wishes. After all, Julie was her only child and she loved her more than anything.

"I do hope I get to meet this great guy soon," she commented. "Maybe the two of you could come down and stay for a long weekend," she added.

"That would be great, Mother. I have to get ready for work now," she said.

"I am happy for you, dear, and I love you very much."

"Thanks, Mom. I love you too," Julie replied.

Julie was glad she had made the call and delighted that her mother trusted her judgment. Poor David, Julie thought, he is going to have to let go of me and get on with his life. Maybe this will motivate him to find a new love of his own.

It was quiet when Matt entered the apartment. Both of his girls were still sleeping. Laura was purring like a kitten when he checked in on her. He was hoping she would stay like that for a little while to give him and Katie some private time to get reacquainted. Despite his earlier activities with Julie, he was ready for more and felt pride in his insatiable sex drive. He tiptoed into the bedroom and undressed and was about to get into bed when Katie stirred and saw him. His tan naked body aroused her, and she immediately reached for him. Her skillful Adonis pleasured her into a passionate delight. Just when they were both about to erupt he mounted her and exploded inside her. They lay back, exhausted, yet exhilarated.

He chuckled and said, "Surprise!"

"I'd like to be surprised like this every morning," she said.

"I'll try to remember that," he promised. "I think I'd better go in and wake the princess."

"By the way, how did you get home? Did Kevin give you a ride?"

"No, actually one of the guys up there loaned me his car for the day. I have to get it back to him tonight."

"That's really sweet of him. Sounds like you made nice friends up there," Katie commented.

"The best," he said as he slipped on his pants.

With that, the bedroom door flew open and in came Laura. "Daddy, Daddy! You're home! I thought I heard your voice!" she cried as she sprang into his arms and wrapped hers around his neck while she smothered him with kisses.

"How is my baby girl?" he asked.

"I'm okay now that you're home!" she said.

"I brought you a little surprise, Princess," he said as he pulled out the dainty heart necklace he had gotten in Quincy Market.

Her eyes opened wide as she exclaimed, "Daddy, it's beautiful. Can you put it on for me, please?" she asked, as she handed it to him. "Oh Daddy, thank you; I'll never take it off," she said just like a real drama queen. "I almost forgot, Daddy; you have to meet Mattie," she cried as she pushed away from him and shimmied down and ran out of the room. Two seconds later, she was back with a green lizard in her hands holding it out for Matt to take. "Daddy, isn't he cute? Look, he's turning tan to match your color. Chameleons change colors to protect themselves when they enter new environments so no one can see what they really are. Did you know that Daddy?" she asked. A moment later, she thoughtfully remarked, "But he was sad too."

"Why's that?" asked Matt.

"He missed his first parade while we were away at the shore," she pouted. Matt looked at Katie as if to ask what Laura could be talking about.

"She's upset she missed the Columbus Day Parade while we were at Ann Marie's beach house," explained Katie.

"Well, we'll have to have our own parade, won't we?" he told her. "Call your little friends and tell them to be over here at two o'clock for the best parade ever."

"Really, Daddy? How can we have our own parade?" she asked.

"I'll show you," he said. "Now go and call your friends and tell them to decorate their bikes and wear colorful clothes."

Katie laughed, "You are such a big kid. I'll make breakfast while you two plan your parade." She started to feel badly about doubting his fidelity. They had never been separated for any length of time before.

The parade started at 2:15 sharp with Matt as the grand marshal leading a parade of five girls. He wore a beefeater's hat from an old Halloween costume and a makeshift sash labeling him grand marshal. But it was the broken broom stick that he used as his marching baton that established his role as leader. The girls decorated their bikes with streamers and flags and wore festive hats from one of Laura's previous parties. They were indeed a colorful sight. A group of people had already assembled as the bizarre entourage proceeded up the block and across the street into the Neighborhood Park and back. The girls beamed as more and more spectators gathered to watch them and clapped in approval, Katie and Ann Marie among them. Once home the girls were excited to celebrate with a cake that Ann Marie had baked this morning for the impromptu occasion, right after Katie had called to inform her of Matt's idea for the parade.

She turned to Matt, "I don't know how you dreamed that parade up, but you made five little girls very happy. Would you like me to take Laura to our house for a while to give you two some time alone together?" Anne Marie asked.

Katie answered, "That would be great, but she won't want to leave her hero, especially knowing he is only here for a few more hours."

"Don't worry; we'll take you up on the offer in a few weeks," Matt said.

After the party dispersed and Matt received his hugs and kisses from the girls, he plopped down into his easy chair. Katie approached Matt from behind and wrapped her arms around his neck and kissed him.

"I just love you so much. Why don't you take a nap while Laura is busy with Mattie, and I'll wake you up when dinner is ready," Katie suggested.

"Sounds great," he said as he closed his eyes in content.

He regretted having to drive back to Connecticut that night; he didn't like leaving his comfort zone even with his considerable ability to adapt wherever he went. After all, growing up as a lonely only child, it never got any easier, especially leaving his two girls.

Only two more weeks, he thought. The traffic made the drive back more stressful, and he knew he wouldn't make it back in time to pick Julie up from work. He was relieved to find her already sleeping when he got in. He was so exhausted that he fell asleep as soon as his head hit the pillow.

MONDAY, OCTOBER 17

Julie awoke to find Matt scurrying out of bed since they had both forgotten to set the alarm, and Jack would be there any minute.

"Oh Matt, I'm so sorry. I tried to stay awake for you last night, but I guess I fell asleep." She found herself following him around as he quickly dressed and freshened up for the day.

"It's okay. I'm fine," he answered.

"But I didn't get to ask you about your family and the wake and all," she said. "Was everyone okay?"

He turned and looked at her strangely before answering, "Everything went well." He quickly gave her a peck on the cheek and darted for the door.

Once outside, he dialed Katie and told her he was back safely and that he missed her and Laura more than ever after seeing them the day before and couldn't wait until his work stint was over. Less than a minute later Jack pulled up and he got in the car and was off to another day of work. Julie was watching from the window with a renewed apprehension.

It was another busy lunch shift for Julie and she just wanted to get home and put her feet up. At least she had the night to herself to regroup while Matt watched the game at Conor's. An unexpected visit from David interrupted her thoughts.

"You look tired, babe," he said, as he kissed her on the cheek.

"I am," she answered. "I'm just about to leave. What's up?"

"I wanted to ask if you would mind if I painted the house when I move in," he lied. He would use any excuse just to see her.

"David, why would you come here to ask, when it will be your house, and you can do as you please with it? Besides, why would you have a problem with the color when you were the one who picked it out in the first place?" She felt a cramp coming on and sat down.

"Are you alright?" he asked.

"I'm fine. I'm just adjusting to an overactive sex life." She wasn't sure why she sometimes made such remarks to him. Maybe she hadn't forgiven him after all for severely disrupting her life earlier. "I'm going to the doctor tomorrow if you must know," she said. David felt a deep pang in his heart at the thought of her being intimate with someone else. Now he knew how she must have felt when she found out that he had cheated on her.

"You *are* using protection, aren't you?" he asked. He stood over her as he stared intently at her and said, "Julie, you may not have to worry about a pregnancy, but for God's sake, you don't even know this guy or who he has been with!" Her glare actually scared him, and he stepped aside to let her pass as she silently stalked away.

Julie tried her hardest to stay awake to see Matt when he came in from his Monday night male bonding at Conor's, but for now, she needed to relax. She was exhausted from an extremely busy day at the Sahara. Her body ached from head to toe, and her back cried for a heating pad but she just didn't have the energy to get up and get it.

Lying on the couch she found herself thinking about her unpleasant conversation with David earlier that afternoon. He had put her in a foul mood for the rest of the day, with his derogatory comments about Matt, a man he didn't even know. She couldn't understand David's biased remarks when he hadn't even met Matt, while anyone who *had* met him considered him to be a pleasant gentleman with impeccable manners and an extremely agreeable disposition. She had to remind herself that David might be jealous and to ignore any future offensive remarks he might make. In fact, she would make it a point to avoid David until he changed his attitude toward Matt. With this thought in mind, she dozed off and began dreaming.

She and Matt were dressed in formal attire for a wedding, though she had no idea whose wedding they were attending. Wearing a black long-tailed tuxedo and a black top hat, Matt resembled a Kennedy with his handsome celebrity looks. Julie wore an elegant off-white Grecian style gown, tastefully adorned in gold. The gown gathered snugly in just the right places, while it draped loosely in others, emphasizing her shapely body. She looked more elegant than any Roman or Greek goddess could have, with her dainty tiara upon her tightly spun chignon. Her diamond teardrop earrings and necklace ensemble sparkled as brightly as her eyes. She and Matt approached what appeared to be revolving doors of a church, and she pushed through first. Once inside she turned to wait for Matt, who should have followed right behind her, but to her surprise, the door just kept spinning faster and faster. Finally, when the door came to an abrupt stop, standing before her was a faceless lizard-like creature in Matt's tuxedo and top hat. And the creature was staring right through her.

She jolted into an upright position sweating profusely with her heart racing. Just then Matt entered the room to find her clammy and slightly disoriented. It took her a minute to realize she had been dreaming. He held her until she was calm while she explained she had just woken from a strange and lucid dream. She wasn't able to articulate her dream to Matt, although she wondered if it meant anything.

She was sure David's earlier negative statements had initiated her dream; therefore, she reaffirmed her decision to avoid him. That night in bed, she clung to Matt as she tried to make sense of her disturbing nightmare.

TUESDAY, OCTOBER 18

Julie awoke to find Matt making breakfast for her. He had wanted to serve her in bed, but the smell of bacon and eggs frying drew her to the kitchen. He gathered her in his arms when he saw her standing beside him and kissed the top of her head.

"How are you feeling this morning?" he asked. She assured him she was fine and that it was only a dream. He was worried maybe she was working too hard and needed some rest, but she again insisted that she was fine as she took over preparing breakfast.

"I know only too well how real nightmares can seem. I've suffered from them since I was a kid," he offered but without referring to any root cause.

"Why didn't you ever wake me up?"" asked a concerned Julie.

He had no intention of elaborating any further about his affliction. Matt looked at the clock. "Oh, I gotta go," he said as he jumped up and ran for the door. He wanted to make a call before Jack came for him.

"Aren't you going to eat something?" she called after him.

"I ate already. I was just making breakfast for you," he shouted back, before closing the door behind him.

"Good morning, beautiful!" Matt said to Katie on the other end of the phone.

She answered, "Oh, Matt, I miss you so much. I just can't wait until this is over."

"Me too, sweetie. We only have two more weeks to go. We can make it. I'm fantasizing about our making up for lost time when I get back."

"I am too," she said. "In fact, Ann Marie has already agreed to take Laura and Mattie for a couple of days so we can be alone."

"Not before I spend some time with her, I hope," said Matt. "I miss her little hugs and kisses."

"Don't worry, I'll give you two your time, and then you are all mine."

"That's a deal. Look, I have to go; Jack just pulled up. Talk to you soon. I love you both."

"Hi Matt," said Jack. "I can't believe you find people to talk to every day at this hour. It must be your morning ritual," he laughed, trying to make light of it. He was curious about Matt's daily cell phone conversations.

"You know how mothers can be if you don't call them," Matt lied. His mom had worked herself to death some years earlier. He never knew how much his mother really loved him until he found her diary. She wasn't demonstrative, and she never got over Matt's father taking off and leaving her with a one-year-old child and with no means of support.

"You're a better son than I am," lauded Jack. "My wife has to remind me to call my mother."

Julie was surprised that she didn't have to wait long in the doctor's office. She was taken into an examination room immediately and asked to disrobe, put on an office gown and wait for the doctor. She loved her family's long time physician, Dr. Schaberg. He was so patient with her and David when they were trying to have a baby. He had referred them to Dr. Landers, an obstetrician, who was a prominent fertility specialist. It made her sad to think about those times in the past. She was happy now, and she wanted to stay that way, she thought as Dr. Schaberg walked in.

"It is so good to see you, Julie. What brings you here today?" he asked.

"Doctor, I think I am coming down with something. I'm fatigued, achy and nauseous lately," she began. She told him about Matt and their frequent sexual activity. "I'm sure it is just the extreme change in routine." She also told him about Matt and their active social lives.

After his examination of her, Dr. Schaberg advised her that he could not find anything wrong with her short of a possible virus and suggested supplemental vitamins and rest.

"Well, I think you should see Dr. Landers to eliminate any other concerns," he suggested, referring to sexually transmitted diseases. He reprimanded her for not using protection, especially with a stranger. How could she explain to him that Matt was never a stranger to her?

"If you don't feel any better otherwise, I want you to make another appointment and we will do a complete physical with further testing."

Dr. Schaberg was extremely fond of Julie and remembered her disappointment the many times she was told that the fertility treatments hadn't worked and she wasn't pregnant. The girl deserved some happiness. Dr. Schaberg had been so disillusioned with David for seeking solace in someone else's arms when Julie needed him most. He hoped this new fellow, Matt, was everything she said he was.

As for Julie, she was relieved that she didn't have an issue that needed to be discussed with Matt. She certainly wasn't going to mention any of this to him. In fact, she was sure she wouldn't need to make an appointment with Dr. Landers as long as the cramping stopped. She was sure it was caused by her infrequent vomiting. She knew that Matt already had enough to think about.

Julie wasn't in the house a minute before the doorbell rang. She wanted to close the door in his face when she saw David outside. She stood with the door open but didn't ask him in.

"David, look, I'm tired and I'm going to lie down," she said.

"I just want to hear about your doctor's appointment," he said in a concerned tone.

"Just what I said, too much great sex," she said. David looked like she had punched him in the stomach. She knew he genuinely cared about her, and yet she was being mean to him again.

"Seriously, I'm fine. Dr. Schaberg didn't notice anything wrong. Thank you for worrying about me, but it's not necessary. Please, I need to rest before Matt comes home."

"Okay. I'll always love you, Julie," he said as he walked away sadly.

Julie usually waited for Matt before starting dinner because she never knew what time he would be getting off work. She wouldn't try to call him since she didn't want him to think that she was checking up on him. It was after ten o'clock when Matt came waltzing in the door. She was disappointed to learn that he had taken Jack to Conor's to meet the crew after work. He was so close, two blocks away, yet so distant from her. Julie had noticed that Matt seemed preoccupied at times since his return from Jersey. She thought it better to leave this issue alone for now. Tonight she had to coax him into lovemaking. He eventually responded to her with excited lust thus dispelling any insecurity she might have had, as she lay contentedly in his arms. Julie learned a long time ago that a woman is better off not asking a man too many questions if any. Men tend to share more on their own when they are ready. She didn't want her curiosity to chase Matt away.

WEDNESDAY, OCTOBER 19, AND THURSDAY, OCTOBER 20

Julie actually had to nudge Matt awake in the morning. He neither heard the alarm clock nor jumped out of bed with the first buzz of the alarm as he usually did. He insisted that he was fine and only a bit tired. He didn't want anything to eat for breakfast but drank his usual cup of freshly brewed coffee. Julie reminded him they would be bowling later that night. He didn't seem as excited as usual but smiled nevertheless. He kissed her on the cheek and walked out to wait for Jack. She wasn't sure what it was that was wrong with Matt; she would have to wait until he said something. Maybe he was catching what she had.

"Hi Matt," Katie said as she answered the phone on the first ring.

"Hi," Matt answered.

"Is everything alright?"

"Yeah. Just a bit tired, that's all," he said. "I think this work is getting to me, and I just can't wait to get home."

"Hey, what happened to Mr. Positive?" she asked.

"He's taking a rest, I guess," he laughed with effort. "I'll be all right. How's the princess?"

"She is always so busy with that chameleon that I'm not having any problems with her at all."

"She's a good little girl. Give her a kiss for me."

"Oh Matt, I almost forgot to tell you that both Mrs. Burg and Mrs. Johnson came to our door to ask about you. They were worried that something had happened to the kind gentleman who carries their packages home for them. I reassured them that you would be home soon. They are two cute little old ladies, aren't they?"

"That they are. Gotta go. Love you." he said, and hung up as Jack pulled up.

The lanes were louder than usual, thought Matt, or maybe it was his imagination. His head felt a bit heavy, and he was more tired than usual, which was not surprising given the long strenuous hours he had been working. He and Julie were assigned to lane three that night with Vinnie and Carol. The honeymooners they were subbing for weren't expected back for another two weeks. While Matt was searching for a house ball to bowl with, some of Julie's league acquaintances approached her to inquire about her handsome new beau. Evidently, they were impressed with him, which pleased her to no end.

Matt struggled from the start with few strikes or spares. Julie noticed his frustration but said nothing, for she had been in that position many times before and knew other bowlers' comments could make things worse. The next two games didn't get any better for him. Although their overall team scores reflected Matt's less-than-stellar performance, at the end of the night, they still managed to win all three games. They bantered less, too, even though their opponents, the Strikers, were fast-witted people. Carol, Vinnie, and Julie took note of the difference in Matt and were not surprised when he wanted to leave right after the last game. Although everyone was disappointed she and Matt didn't stay for a drink, Julie thought it best they go home. She had noticed that he was pinching his sinuses from time to time.

"Are you all right?" she asked him.

"I'm fine," he lied. Matt never complained because no one listened to him when he was growing up. His mother always told him that with two jobs, she didn't have time for his trivial concerns. Julie knew something didn't seem right with Matt, but she just couldn't pinpoint it.

Matt's problem became quite apparent the next morning when he couldn't get out of bed or even lift his head off the pillow. He described the symptoms as flulike.

"I think I have sinusitis," he said. "It happens every year. I'll be okay once I get an antibiotic into me." Julie insisted on getting someone to cover for her at work so she could get him to a doctor. She also called Jack who understood and advised Julie that he did not want Matt to feel any pressure to return to work before he was able.

It wasn't easy getting Matt from the bed to the car, but Julie managed to maneuver Matt's dead weight. She was glad there wasn't a long wait at the urgent care since Matt was ghostly pale and kept nodding off and falling into her lap. She was relieved when the doctor corroborated Matt's prognosis of sinusitis and assured her that with an antibiotic he would be himself within two days. Julie picked up his prescription and made him take it before he nodded off again. Julie watched over Matt all day and night and updated Jack on Matt's condition.

Julie awoke earlier this morning without waking Matt. She went downstairs to organize his needs for the day since she had to work a double shift and she wouldn't be home with him. She prepared his breakfast of hot oatmeal and coffee and brought it up to him. He was so weak that she had to wake him so she could feed him. She told him that she was leaving soup in the refrigerator for him to microwave for lunch and plenty of orange and cranberry juices. He was barely aware of her presence as he fell back to sleep. She thought it wise to leave a note reminding him about the soup and juices along with her telephone number at the Sahara. She tried unsuccessfully to get someone to cover her shifts. She hated leaving Matt alone but she had no choice.

She ran into the Sahara at the last minute and did her setup work faster than she had ever done it before. Dennis was already behind the bar after doing his setup. Julie told Dennis the situation with Matt, how she'd reluctantly left him sick at the house; Dennis agreed to watch her tables while she ran home and checked on him in between her shifts.

A fire alarm interrupted their lunch shift, and everyone went running out of the restaurant. The fire trucks pulled up, but after a thorough search of the restaurant, the firefighters found only a faulty wire that was smoking. Had the wire not been found, the entire restaurant could have been reduced to ashes. Dennis and Julie were both relieved as everyone was escorted back into the now-safe building. Julie's two tables weren't at all upset by the near catastrophe. The two elderly retired couples welcomed any sort of excitement into their lives and couldn't wait to share this "adventure" at the next senior citizens' gathering.

Julie and Dennis laughed at the craziness of the whole event. Lunch had started out smoothly just like any day and the next minute the sirens from four neighboring towns were wailing outside their door.

"Never a dull moment," Dennis said.

"I have enough excitement right now, thank you," Julie said. She made sure she had everything set up for the dinner shift before running home to check on Matt.

She found Matt looking and feeling better and sitting up in bed reading the paper when she walked in. He could at least get himself out of bed and into the bathroom. Julie had brought him some roasted chicken and mashed potatoes from the restaurant, plus she made him some coffee and refreshed his drinks before she returned to the Sahara. But first, she quickly gave him the rundown of her morning crisis. He was shocked but glad that the emergency hadn't been any worse than a smoldering wire. She kissed his head and ran for the door, intending to return to her nursing duties right after her shift.

Dennis had everything under control as Julie rushed in to start her second shift. He had already served her table their drinks and salads after taking their dinner orders.

"How is Matt?" Dennis asked.

"Much better," she said. "Thanks so much for helping me out again. I don't know what I would do without you."

"Do you think we can just get through the night without any further excitement?" Dennis asked.

Julie laughingly answered, "I do hope so." With that, the front door opened and the dinner rush began. Julie and Dennis began their frantic routine of dashing back and forth. Julie gave Jack a quick smile when she noticed him sitting at the bar.

At the end of her shift, Julie went over to Jack to give him an update on Matt and said she wasn't sure if he'd be up to working in the morning. Jack's main concern was Matt's health. He knew Matt was the kind of guy who would return to work as soon as he was able. He wasn't one to take advantage of the system. When it came to Julie, though, Jack wasn't as sure about Matt's actions. He tried to think of a way to ask Julie if Matt was treating her right, but since he couldn't, he simply left it alone. He really hoped he was wrong about his gut feeling when it came to Matt's relationship with Julie, but judging by Matt's behavior, he sincerely doubted it. She said good night to all, as she left to return to her nursing duties.

Matt's doctor had correctly predicted that Matt would be feeling better by that night. When Julie walked into the house, she found Matt cooking in the kitchen.

"What are you doing out of bed, Mister?" she asked sternly.

"I'm making our dinner for tomorrow night," he said. "It sounds like my Florence Nightingale has turned into a Nurse Ratched. Seriously, that sinusitis threw me for a loop."

"How often do you get it?" she asked.

"At least once a year. It usually comes without warning. Sinusitis always kicks my butt."

"Well, I'm gonna kick your handsome butt if you don't get back to bed," she said sternly.

"Okay, okay," he said. "Can you put the chili away for tomorrow?"

"I must say it does smell wonderful." Julie found herself more and more intrigued with Matt. He was just unbelievable.

FRIDAY, OCTOBER 21

The next morning Matt was up and about getting ready for work. He insisted that he felt one hundred percent better.

"Promise me you'll come right home from work and rest," Julie said adamantly.

"Aren't we going with the Conor's crowd on the haunted hayride tonight?" he asked.

"I don't think that's a good idea. You need your rest."

"I'm fine and we *are* going tonight," he insisted. "Just wait until I get you alone in one of those haystacks," he said as he winked at her and walked out the door.

"You'd better dress warmly then. Hey, wait a minute; you forgot my kiss," she shouted to a closed front door.

Julie noticed that today Matt was pacing outside the house at a much slower rate.

"Hello there," Matt started off.

"What do you mean, 'Hello there,' Katie snorted. "I haven't heard from you since Wednesday! Matt, I want to know what's going on with you."

"I'm sorry, honey, but I was so sick in bed with sinusitis. You know how badly I get it, and I didn't want you to worry."

"Not calling worries me! You know that I would have come up and brought you home or at least taken care of you up there if I had known. Ann Marie would have watched Laura."

"I'm okay, and I wouldn't have wanted you to leave Laura. Believe me, I'm fine. By the way, I won't be coming home tomorrow," he said casually.

"If I didn't know you any better, I'd think there was something on up there!"

"Katie, you *do* know me better than that. Look, we're trying to tie up loose ends here so we can go home next week," he lied. "Just think, babe, in less than a week we'll be together again. Sorry, but I have to go; my ride is here. I love you," he said as he quickly hung up.

Jack was quick to say, "Are you being a mama's boy again?"

"Huh?" Matt looked at him in a confused manner, not remembering his lie to Jack earlier that week. A moment later, Matt recalled telling Jack about his daily chats with his mother. "As an only child, I feel obligated to call."

"You really are a good son! By the way, how are you feeling after that sinus infection you had?" Jack asked with genuine concern.

"I'm back to myself," he said. He told Jack how Julie had practically carried him in and out of the doctor's office because he was so weak.

"Well, you bounced back quickly in two days. It's amazing what a little TLC can do for a man."

"She was more like Nurse Ratched," Matt complained. Jack was amazed that Matt spoke disparagingly about Julie, despite all the love and attention she gave him.

As soon as Matt got home, Julie suggested that he rest while she prepared rice for the chili Matt had made the night before, and then they could head out to Conor's. He insisted on taking a shower first. She could hear him singing his own rendition of *'The Monster Mash'*.

"*They did the mash, they did the monster mash, it was a graveyard smash, they did the mash: they did the monster mash...*"

Oh, what a night this is going to be, she thought. She enjoyed the childlike sense of adventure she saw in Matt. He was refreshing and fun.

Matt and Julie thought the scene at Conor's was quite comical when they walked in. The women were at one end of the bar organizing the gang's road trip while the men were at the other end debating the outcome of the upcoming weekly football games. One would think they had a crystal ball with the capability of predicting the teams' wins and losses. Julie went to her respective side of the bar while Matt went to his. One drink turned into two drinks before the two groups agreed upon their final plan. Chris had a van that could comfortably seat eight people and was more than happy to be the designated driver since he was drinking soda that night. The crew climbed into the van and started out on their excursion. They were more like a bunch of kids going on a class trip than adults going on a haunted hayride.

While the others were waiting in the long line for tickets, Matt strayed from them unnoticed. He had always had a compulsive need to explore his surroundings. He found a shed a short distance from the hayride queue and decided to look inside. It was too dark to see so he stepped inside and tried to feel along the wall for the light switch as the door shut behind him, locking him in. When Matt tried to push the door open again, he found that the latch was on the outside.

Matt beat on the door and screamed frantically but could not be heard over the extremely loud, eerie Halloween music. He groped around to find something that he could use to pry open the door, but all he felt were sharp jagged objects. He began to sweat profusely as his shouts went unheard. Then he sank to the ground shaking and crying as he began slipping into a delusional state.

"Mommy, Mommy, please don't lock me in here. I promise I'll be a good boy, and I won't touch anything. I'll stay in my bed and I'll go right to sleep. I promise, Mommy, but please don't lock me in here tonight; I'm scared of the dark." Through his sobs, he imagined his mother's reply.

"Matthew, don't make it any worse than it is. You know I have to go to work, and I can't afford a babysitter. I know you'll be safe in there. Just lie down on your pillow and blankets and go to sleep and when you wake up, I will be home and it will be light outside."

"No, Mommy, don't go. Please don't leave me alone in here," he pleaded as his chest heaved in convulsive sobs. "Mommy, Mommy, help me!" he screamed as he heard the front door of their apartment close. Matt began to hyperventilate and then collapsed.

During a brief pause in the Halloween noise soundtrack, a child passing by the shed thought he heard shouts coming from within and reported his suspicions to the first employee he could find. The worker, of course, thought the child had an overactive imagination given the ominous environment but agreed to check inside the shed to satisfy the boy's concern. When he opened the shed and turned on the light, he found Matt curled up in a fetal position in the corner soaked in blood and perspiration.

By now, Julie and the rest of their friends had been searching for Matt for over thirty minutes. She headed toward the crowd of people assembled around the shed hoping to find Matt among them but was shocked to see that Matt was the attraction. Julie gasped at the pathetic sight of Matt with his hands bleeding profusely from grasping the sharp tools in the dark. When he spotted her through the crowd, he sprang up and ran into her arms.

"Oh, Mommy, you came back for me," he cried as he clung to her so tightly she could hardly breathe. He was like a lost child who had experienced severe separation anxiety and was reunited with his mother after he was found. She assumed he was disoriented from being alone in the dark because, of course, she was unaware of his childhood trauma. The EMT on site bandaged Matt's superficial wounds, but he was oblivious to and was not qualified to tend to the emotional scars from Matt's past that had been torn open when that shed door closed.

Matt had calmed down considerably by the time the rest of the gang found them, which saved him the embarrassment of giving a detailed explanation, but he still would not let go of Julie. They all thought it best to abort their trip and to get Matt home as soon as possible. Julie was convinced that Matt had not fully recuperated from his sinusitis and held it responsible for his anxiety attack. She thought, we both certainly have had our ills lately; at least my cramps have subsided. Matt's thoughts were focused on how the earlier horror had reminded him of the reason he had a constant need for companionship as Julie held and soothed him.

Once home and in bed, Matt clung to Julie and almost in a whimper said, "I thought you would never find me."

She soothed him to sleep like a mother would a frightened child.

SATURDAY, OCTOBER 22

Julie was stunned when Matt jumped out of bed the next day as if nothing had happened the night before. She didn't want to embarrass him by mentioning it.

"What's on the agenda for today?" he asked.

"I think you need to take it easy, Matt," she said with great concern. "You've had a bad week," she said referring to his sinusitis, which she believed caused the disturbing incident last night.

"Anyway, I have to go food shopping after work so I may not be here when you get home," she continued.

"Look, today is Saturday, and Jack usually lets us off early. Can you please wait for me to go with you?" he asked. "I love to food shop. I just want to be with you. That's all," he said in a pleading way. She couldn't resist his boyish manner when he said that.

"Alright," she conceded. "I'll wait for you, but if you aren't feeling well, you don't have to come."

"That's a deal. Thank you" he said as he gave her a big hug and kiss on the cheek. Watching him walk out the door, Julie couldn't help thinking, what man likes to go food shopping?

"Good morning, my love," Matt said into the phone. "Well, it's almost over, and this time next week I'll be waking you up in person in a much more intimate way."

"You hung on me so quickly yesterday," Julie snapped.

"Please don't start on me. It's been an awful week," he gritted through his teeth.

"I'm sorry, I can't wait until you come home, and neither can your greatest fan. She is so excited. She walks around the house talking to Mattie about you and telling him everything the three of you are going to be doing together."

"What about you? Aren't you included?" he asked.

"No, thank you! She knows I'm not particularly fond of chameleons."

"Why did you buy it for her then?" he asked.

"It looked at her. That's why!" she exclaimed.

"It *looked* at her?" he asked, trying to understand.

"She said it looked at her with sad *puppy* eyes like yours, and she thought it must be missing someone too. Hence our new family member," she told him. He began to laugh just thinking of Laura saying this. He missed her, too.

"Honey, I can't remember if I told you that I won't be home tomorrow, but we want to get everything in order before we leave. Anyway, it's only a matter of days now, right?"

"I guess so, but it will be the longest week ever."

"Here comes Jack; I'll call you tomorrow. Love you," he said as he quickly hung up without waiting for a response.

"What in God's name happened to your hands?" Jack cried as Matt got into the car. He had noticed Matt's hands, which were all scratched and bandaged from his escapade in the shed the night before.

"I was playing with a cat," he lied, his face flushing.

"What kind of cat was it, a tiger?"

Julie was happy to hear Nancy's voice on the other end of the phone and not David's. He had become even more of a nuisance lately with his calls and unexpected visits. She felt that his concern—not to mention his jealousy—was totally unnecessary. She'd always thought that they would remain friends, but now his attitude toward Matt made her question that possibility.

"Hello, Julie," said Nancy. "I'm calling to invite you to a small dinner party that I'm throwing tonight. I thought you might like to come and show off your new beau. I'm inviting only a few intimate friends. You know most of them—John with Sue, Amanda with Nick, and Lynn with Michael. It's an interesting mix, don't you think?" she asked.

"To say the least," Julie agreed. "I'd love to come, but I won't have an answer for you until Matt gets home."

"Why don't you just call him and ask him?" Nancy questioned.

"There's no need to since he gets off early today so I don't have to bother him at work." She quickly added, "I wouldn't want him to get electrocuted while answering a call from me." Julie was not about to explain that she had never called Matt; in fact, she didn't even know his telephone number. She had promised herself that she was not going to be pushy and she would wait for him to give it to her if it was necessary. She still strongly felt that she would not call him, short of an emergency.

"Alright. Let me know as soon as you can so I can prepare for two more," Nancy said.

To Julie's delight, Matt was not only excited about the dinner party but he was also eager to meet new people.

"I'll call Nancy and tell her to expect us later, while you take your shower."

"You mean you didn't accept the invitation right away?" he questioned, evidently shocked.

"No, I didn't want to take the liberty of accepting on your behalf without asking you first," she explained, "although, I did lay out our clothes just in case."

"That's why I think you are such a doll," he said as he took her in his arms, hugged her, and kissed the top of her head.

"Hurry into the shower if you still feel up to going shopping with me," she told him.

Shopping with Matt turned out to be an adventure for Julie. She was amazed to see what an avid food shopper he was.

"You seem to have had a lot of practice at this," she said.

"I've been shopping forever," he said. "That was one of my chores as a kid. My father left my mother years ago and since it was only us two, and she worked two jobs, I picked up some of the domestic duties as I got older." Of course, he never mentioned shopping was a weekly date that he also enjoyed with Katie.

"It must have been rough for you as an only child with no one to share the burden." He ignored her remark and continued shopping ahead of her, obviously not wanting to talk about it any further. Matt had always wondered what it would have been like if his father hadn't left, and if his mother would have been happier and shown him more affection.

Julie was sorry she took him down the canned goods aisle because he began juggling the cans up in the air—two, three, then four—while crowds were gathering around to watch. Julie thought to herself, no wonder he likes to go shopping; he can do all the juggling he wants in the aisles and be guaranteed an audience.

On the way home, they stopped to pick up a bottle of wine to bring to Nancy's.

"Do you mind if I don't go into the store with you?" Matt asked. "I haven't talked to Kevin for a while and I just want to catch up with him," said Matt.

"That's fine. I can manage," she said as she opened the door and stepped out of the car. He dialed Kevin right away and was relieved when he got his voicemail. It was so much easier to leave a message explaining that he wouldn't need a ride home tomorrow because Jack had something for him to do than to get stuck having to answer any questions Kevin might pose to him.

When they got home, it was almost time to get ready to leave for Nancy's, so they both put the groceries away and went upstairs to get dressed. Julie had laid out gray slacks for Matt with a collared light blue shirt and his navy blue sports jacket. She was going to wear a tight-fitting midnight blue mini dress with her navy colored pumps and a matching purse. They both took one glance at each other and Matt made a move toward her, but she quickly said,

"Matt, not now, we'll be late, but I promise we'll have all the time in the world when we get home." She recognized that animal look in his eyes and wanted more than anything to engage him, but now just wasn't the time. She didn't want to be late for Nancy's, and she wanted to make a grand entrance, just like Cinderella and her Prince Charming.

Nancy greeted Matt and Julie at the door and immediately put her arm in his as she escorted him away from Julie into the living room.

"You really *are* a dreamboat," Nancy purred.

"Thank you for the compliment," Matt answered sheepishly as he looked back to see if Julie was following. Julie was amused by the way Nancy maneuvered Matt into the center of the room to make her general announcement:

"I would like everyone to meet Julie's new friend, Matt. He's from New Jersey and is on loan to our local power company."

"Welcome, Matt," they all shouted at him, as Julie joined him at his side. She was glad that Nancy had referred to Matt as her friend, knowing how sensitive he was to people's assumptions about their relationship. She felt sure that the more comfortable that he became with her, the greater the chance that he would share his intentions. Matt took it all in stride and responded to Nancy's spontaneous introduction with smiles. It actually was a clever ploy on Nancy's part to break the ice and make Matt feel welcome.

"Hi, Matt. I'm John. So what is it that you actually do for the power company?" he asked.

"I'm a linesman," Matt answered.

"I'm a 'sparkie' myself," offered John. Matt chuckled at the term often used for an electrician. John, the benevolent fellow that he was, asked Matt if he was interested in living in Connecticut, and if so, he would hook him up with potential electrical and power jobs since he was well connected.

"Thanks," said Matt. "I'll keep that in mind."

Julie's attention was diverted by Sue, John's wife.

"I'm so happy for you, Julie, but I do have to tell you that I still have a big soft spot for David," she said.

"I can understand that," said Julie. "I still have a close friendship with him."

"Is he all right with this?" Sue asked, referring to Julie's new love.

"He's coming around to it, but he really has no choice now, does he?"

"I don't know if Nancy told you or not, but she had invited David tonight, and he declined. He said he didn't want to make you and Matt feel uncomfortable. I think that is very chivalrous of him, don't you?" she asked. Before Julie could answer, Amanda interrupted them to say hello to Julie. Amanda was John and Sue's newly married daughter and had known Julie for as long as she could remember. Their other daughter, Danielle, was a special education teacher but was on a date, so couldn't make the dinner party. John and Sue were rightfully proud of their two beautiful intelligent daughters. Julie loved to watch the way Amanda and her father interacted; seeing them together reminded her of the special relationship she once had with her own father.

When Julie looked over toward Matt, she saw that Sue and John's new son-in-law Nick had joined Matt and John in conversation. Nick worked for another power company in Connecticut, so he and Matt talked shop about the struggles they had experienced in the last couple of weeks following the nor'easter. Nick told an animated tale of how he was splicing lines when a huge tree limb fell on the swivel so hard it jerked him right out of the truck's bucket. Funny as he made it seem, he knew he was lucky to be alive. Matt chuckled remembering how something similar had happened to his buddy, Tommy. Only it was Billy who had started driving away and forgotten that Tommy was in the bucket. Julie joined the group just as Nancy announced that dinner was being served and she needed everyone to take their places. Julie sat to Matt's left, while Lynn sat to his right. Lynn introduced herself to him, as her husband Michael reached past her to extend his hand to Matt.

Lynn asked Matt, "Where are you from in New Jersey?"

"Hoboken," he answered.

"Hoboken! That's where our daughter lives," she squealed in excitement. "What a coincidence! She just loves it there and so do we. We go down whenever we get the chance." Now Michael leaned forward to talk to Matt,

"Where do you live? Our daughter Melissa lives on Hudson Street, three blocks from the Hudson River, right across from the park that is there."

Matt felt his stomach sink as he lied, "Oh, I live on the other side of town closer to Jersey City."

Now the whole table was engrossed in listening to this conversation as Lynn went on to say, "Our daughter told us the cutest story. Last week, she was in the park across the street from her apartment. A father acted as a grand marshal and led five little girls on their decorated bicycles in a parade around the park. The whole neighborhood came out to watch it as they clapped and cheered. How adorable is that?"

"A lot of eccentric things happen in Hoboken," he said, rather sharply, causing Julie to look at him quizzically.

At this point, Matt worried that Lynn and Michael's daughter Melissa not only lived on the same street as he and Katie but also very possibly on the same block, maybe even in the same building. A group of young women had recently moved into the fourth floor of their brownstone.

"I spend more time in Jersey City than Hoboken," he again lied. But before they could respond, he feigned a headache and Julie felt obligated to take him home giving the excuse he was having a sinusitis relapse. She explained how ill he had been recently and after a quick farewell, the stunning couple left.

Julie did not know what to think when Matt suddenly became frisky when they got home. He wrapped his naked body around hers as soon as she got into bed and turned out the light. His headache seemed to have disappeared.

SUNDAY, OCTOBER 23, LITCHFIELD

What a lovely Sunday morning, thought Julie happily as she lay in bed. The full night of lovemaking had been absolutely incredible. Matt entered the bedroom carrying a tray of coffee and waffles for her after letting her sleep later than usual. She never thought she would ever find anyone who could treat her so well again. There were times when David had served her breakfast in bed, but that was a long time ago. She had finally found a man who loved her in the right ways. She knew Matt had to be thinking about how they would work out their long-distance relationship, and she was just waiting for his proposal.

They had such a wonderful time last night with her friends, and she was so proud to be the woman on his arm. She received compliments all night about what a handsome couple they made. She could only imagine what it would be like to walk down the aisle with him.

Nancy had outdone herself not only with the choice of her dinner menu but also her choice of guests, thought Julie. Matt was so comfortable with John and Nick since they shared the same occupations and enjoyed talking shop together. The three of them were so funny telling their outrageous tales from work. Then there were Lynn and Michael who were so excited when they realized that Matt lived in Hoboken. What a coincidence that was! Julie found their story endearing, the story that their daughter had told them, about the father who'd made a parade for his daughter and her little friends. What a thoughtful unique idea! Julie's own father would have been capable of doing something like that. He was always creating something out of the ordinary to entertain her. She recalled fondly that he had once whittled a set of wooden dolls for her and then they had both painted clothes on them. She felt an ache in her heart for her dad since she hadn't thought of him in this way for a very long time.

It was too bad that Matt had a relapse during dinner. She felt responsible since he really should have stayed home and rested up after work the last couple of nights. Both nights ended up being too much for him. Maybe she shouldn't have mentioned anything to him about the dinner party in the first place, but she so wanted to socialize with him, just as Nancy had said, "To show him off". He would never have said no to the social gathering so it wouldn't have mattered if she had suggested staying home and have a quiet night or not.

As though he was reading her mind, Matt said, "I am so glad we went last night. I really had a great time."

"You don't think it was too much for you, too soon after your illness?" she asked.

"Not at all. We left when I felt I had enough, so don't you worry your pretty head," he said as he kissed her. She felt so relieved that he had said that.

"Do we have anything on the agenda for today?" he asked.

"I'm working later, and I do have a few things to do around here first," she said.

"Like what?" he asked.

"To start, I have the laundry to do."

He quickly answered, "It's all done washed, folded and put away."

"Well, I also wanted to vacuum and sweep the floors."

He answered, "The vacuuming is done, and the floors are mopped also.

She just stared at him in shock, and then uttered,

"Wow, you're magical."

"I'm a regular Mary Poppins, at your service."

"Seriously, Matt, when did you have time to get all this done?"

"I woke up very early and couldn't get back to sleep, so thought I might as well make myself useful!"

"Well, you certainly did! Now we have plenty of time to enjoy the day. What kind of adventure did you have in mind?"

"We could take a ride around and see if any of the historical places in nearby Litchfield are open," he said. "We might get lucky."

"Sounds fine to me," she said as she sipped the last of her coffee and Matt lifted the tray from her lap. "I guess since you've seen to the housework, I'll just get ready to go." He leaned over and gave her a lingering kiss as she tried to get out of the bed. While she was in the shower, Julie kept thinking how lucky she was to have met someone so genuinely thoughtful.

Some of the sites were open conveniently using oil lamps to provide lighting as well as the ambience of the colonial past. They went to the Litchfield History Museum, where he learned that Benjamin Franklin's son, William, was a loyalist, unlike his patriot father, and was jailed in a prison that was located in a sequestered area in Litchfield. Matt recalled that Kevin had mentioned that loyalist prisoners were kept there because of Litchfield's location. They also visited the Judge Tapping Reeve House and America's first law school. It was amusing to see how small the desks for law students had been back then, compared to those of today. Julie went into fits of laughter when Matt sat in one of the desks and couldn't get out of it.

"Looks like you are going to become a perpetual student whether you like it or not," she roared. After several unsuccessful attempts, she had to get the security guard to help free him. The thought of his impulsive dilemma left Julie chuckling all day. Despite the humorous drama, they continued on and visited the house were Ethan Allen stayed and the home where Harriett Beecher Stowe grew up.

What began as a romantic lunch on the Village Green resulted in a playful tryst, when Matt threatened to make love to her right then and there. She pushed away from him and began running until he caught her and tackled her to the ground and the two began kissing passionately. Passers-by appeared amused by the two lovers who were overtly enjoying each other.

Before they knew it, it was time for Julie to go to work. Matt was quite satisfied with his tour of Litchfield. He decided to stay at home and watch the Sunday football games until Julie returned from the Sahara. It wasn't long after she left the house that Matt called Katie.

"Hi sweetie," he said.

"Hello, handsome!" she answered. "You're *calling* at a strange time."

"I'm with the guys at a bar with cell service watching the game," he lied. "How's the princess?"

"She's fine! I'm being tortured about your homecoming party."

"Don't fuss. You know the kind of party I want from you when I get home."

"Don't worry; that goes without saying. The fireworks will be flying at *that* party," she promised. "Oh, here comes your party planner now," said Katie, as Laura came bouncing into the room shouting and grabbing for the phone.

"Is that my Daddy? Today starts the countdown, only five more days 'til your party."

He answered her in excitement, "I can't wait. And do you know what I want my present to be? You!"

Through her giggles, Laura said, "I'm gonna have Mommy wrap me up for you, Daddy! I'm going to play with Mattie now. Remember, five more days!"

Katie came back on the line. "How am I going to manage five more days with her?"

"It'll go fast, honey. I'm going to watch the games now. I'll call you tomorrow. I love you."

"Here too," she answered.

After the games, Matt lay on the couch, falling asleep and thinking with a feeling of relief about the two parties that awaited him at home. Julie didn't bother to wake him when she found him so peaceful, so she covered him and went to bed alone.

MONDAY, OCTOBER 24

In the morning Julie could hear Matt singing in the shower, *"Just another manic Monday, wish it were Sunday…"* He was always so happy in the morning, which seemed to energize her for the day. She had nothing to do today except maybe shop since Matt had done all her chores the day before. Maybe she would just lounge around until it was time for work. She would pick Matt up at Conor's after the Monday Night Football.

Jack was a bit early today so Matt didn't have time to make his daily check-in call.

"Looks like you'll be heading back to Jersey at the end of this week," he said. "Things should be wrapped up by then, and they want to let the out-of-towners go home. I'm sure you'll be glad to get back."

"Yeah, it's been a long run," Matt answered.

"Well, it looks like you've enjoyed plenty of our New England hospitality," remarked Jack, who was trying to prompt some conversation regarding Matt's intentions toward Julie.

"I sure did," said Matt, "but there is no place like home." Jack was disappointed Matt didn't even allude to Julie at all, but he knew better than to ask what Matt's plans were.

Matt bounded into Conor's geared up for the game even though neither of the local teams, the Jets or Giants, were playing. Regardless, the swearing, hissing, and hollering still resonated from the Monday Night Quarterbacks. The San Francisco 49ers played the Philadelphia Eagles. Allie was amazed at how fickle the men were; even when their favorite teams weren't playing, they seemed to arbitrarily pick alternate favorites. The Eagles trampled the 49ers with a score of 28-0 making for a quick game and an early night.

Bobby had finally won a football pool and was happy to buy a round of drinks for the crew. Matt called the Sahara and left a message for Julie that he would be walking home so there was no need for her to stop at Conor's.

Nothing seemed to faze Julie, not even David's unexpected visit to the Sahara. She was in a fantasy world of her own.

"Hello Julie," he said as he kissed her cheek. "Do I get to meet Prince Charming tonight?" he asked

"No, sorry, but he isn't here. He's watching the game with the guys at Conor's."

"Am I ever going to meet your Casanova?" he teased, as he internally fumed at the thought that the creep not only had taken his place with Julie but that he also replaced him at Conor's.

"Oh, really, I have no time for you right now. I have work to do," she said and walked away from him as happily as before his visit.

She was very disappointed to find Matt asleep again when she got home. She wanted so much to discuss where their future relationship stood. Although she longed for him tonight, she couldn't bring herself to wake him up.

TUESDAY, OCTOBER 25

The next morning, Julie woke up to Matt blowing in her ear and immediately became aroused. She loved their morning romps, which energized her for the day. Afterward, she went downstairs to make their breakfast while Matt jumped into the shower. Matt was just as cheerful as ever as he spun Julie around the kitchen in a tango dance, then dipped her and kissed her fervently before lifting her back up.

"What do you think about having a cozy night at home tonight?" asked Julie. "We could have pizza and a bottle of wine and maybe rent a movie?"

"That sounds like a plan," he said. He danced out the door and waited at the curb for his ride as he dialed his cell phone.

"Hi Daddy, three more days till you get your present! I don't want you to go away anymore 'cause I miss you too much," she ordered.

With that pronouncement, Katie took the phone from Laura and said, "Me too. She is so excited that I don't know how I am going to manage living with her for the next three days. I missed your daily call yesterday. "

"It'll go fast, Katie," he said ignoring her last statement. "I gotta go, Jack is pulling up. I love you!"

Julie had ulterior motives for wanting to spend a night alone with Matt. Except for their time in bed, they didn't really have much time alone. Since they were always with people either at the Sahara or Conor's, they never really discussed any future plans. She made no demands and asked no questions because she wanted him to take the initiative. He was demonstratively affectionate and sensitive to her needs, which made him seem so close, and yet he was so distant. She knew their time would soon be coming to an end and really wanted to know where she stood with him. Maybe tonight with no social interruptions they could talk. Julie was frustrated about the uncertainty of her future.

In addition to her usual Tuesday routine, Julie added shopping for a bottle of wine and renting a movie. She searched the shelves for the exact movie she wanted. She was so excited about tonight that she didn't see David as he walked toward her on the street even though she wanted to avoid him after their last chance meeting.

"Hello, gorgeous, how about a cup of coffee with an old friend? Remember that Girl Scout jingle, 'Make new friends but keep the old, one is silver and the other is gold.'"

"I'm sorry, but not today. I'm really in a rush to get home. Matt and I are having a quiet night in."

"Isn't he due to leave soon?" he asked.

"He hasn't said anything yet. Anyway, that doesn't make any difference. We can still have a long-distance relationship. I'm taking it one day at a time."

"Julie, I really miss you. Maybe you'll have time for me soon. I'll be waiting for a call from you," he said, giving her a hug and a peck on the cheek as she rushed off. He looked after her wondering how she would respond once she found out the truth about her so-called gentleman, Matt.

David had done the unthinkable and investigated on his own only to find that Matt was supposedly happily married to a beautiful woman and had an adorable five-year-old daughter waiting for him in Hoboken, New Jersey. David was furious and wanted to beat the life out of Matt, but he knew he could never let on to Julie that he knew any of this. She would have reminded him that he had cheated on her and probably would never talk to him again. He carefully considered the situation and decided he would try to keep as close an eye on Julie as possible without becoming an annoyance. He expected Matt to tell her any day now that it was over, which would leave her devastated. David planned on being there to pick up the pieces. He wanted to protect her because he had learned the hard way just how much Julie meant to him.

Julie had everything in order by the time Matt walked in from work. She had dimmed the lights, lit the candles, opened the wine to breathe, and left the pizza warming in the oven. He had forgotten about their plans for the night, but he knew he owed it to her. After all, he would be leaving Friday, but just couldn't bring himself to tell her it was over. She approached him in a very sexy dress and stood on her tiptoes to give him a welcome home kiss. The scent of her perfume overpowered him as he let his hands roam her body, but she pulled away in a teasing manner.

"We'll have time for that later. Let's eat first. The table's set up in the den so we can eat there while we watch the movie."

"Sounds great to me. Let me just wash up, and I'll be right in."

As he was walking toward the bathroom, his cell phone rang, and he instinctively answered it without looking at the caller identification first to see who it was.

"Hello," he said nonchalantly.

"Hello, Daddy," he heard and quickly hung up the phone and shut it off for the night. He was upset with himself for being so careless. He knew Laura would be calling back thinking they were disconnected. He would have to take care of that tomorrow, he thought, as he walked into the bathroom.

Julie was lounging on the roomy sofa in a seductive position holding her glass of wine to her lips when he walked into the den.

"This certainly does look cozy. What movie did you get for us to watch tonight?"

"Your favorite, of course!" Matt looked at her quizzically, not sure how she would know he loved *On the Waterfront*. She reminded him of his previous conversation with Dennis. He had forgotten that she had been there. He appreciated the gesture and her thoughtfulness, but this was his and Katie's movie.

As the movie began, he found his thoughts returning to Hoboken. Katie and he had enjoyed re-enacting some of the scenes as Edie Doyle and Terry Malloy. His favorite was where Edie finds Terry on his apartment rooftop tending to his pigeons. He remembered how he and Katie had travelled along the rooftops and the many times they had made love up there. He could relate to Terry Malloy who was morally saved by Edie. Didn't Katie keep him on the straight and narrow? She was *his* Edie who had saved him from drowning in more ways than one. She protected him and understood him like no one else did. He couldn't wait to find his way back to her and never stray again. He found his resolution comforting as he dozed off in Julie's arms.

Meanwhile, Julie found herself watching the movie alone. She was enchanted with Hoboken but wondered what it was like now and if she would mind living there. From what she researched on her own, it had become more of a yuppie town providing young professionals easy access to New York City, especially with the revival of the ferry system between New York and New Jersey. The waterfront supposedly was renovated and looked nothing like the 1954 movie she was watching. It had parks with wide paved walking and biking paths along the water as well as a breath-taking view of New York. It would be a drastic change for her but she felt life with Matt would be worth it.

Julie was disappointed that Matt didn't share any of his thoughts or intentions with her. She was hoping the movie might have prompted something from him. The night did not go as planned but there would be other opportunities; after all, he was tired from work. When she couldn't wake him to go up to bed, she covered him with a blanket and gave him a motherly kiss on his cheek before retiring herself. She would definitely broach the subject of their future in the morning. She had suffered enough suspense! Could she have made more of this relationship than he? She had never enjoyed a companion as much as Matt.

WEDNESDAY, OCTOBER 26

Matt found Julie sitting at the kitchen table with her cup of coffee and his breakfast waiting for him.

"Good morning, handsome," she said.

"I'm surprised you're talking to me after I fell asleep on you last night. I know you put a lot of effort into making a nice night for us, but I was so tired that I couldn't keep my eyes open. I'll try to make it up to you," he said.

"I'm going to hold you to that," she said. "I enjoyed the movie. I think I would like living in Hoboken."

He quickly changed the subject with, "I can't wait for bowling tonight. I have a lot to make up for after last week's disaster."

"Everyone is entitled to a bad night, Matt. Anyway, you were really sick, but we just didn't know it. My motto is 'Just pick yourself up and start over,' and forget what happened in the past," she said.

"Profound words of advice you speak, my love," he said as he bent over to kiss her on the cheek.

"Is that all you have for me?" she asked as though she were insulted.

"I have a lot more than that, but you'll have to wait until tonight," he said in a playful manner.

"I can't wait," she said as she stood up. Before she could walk to the sink, he twirled her around, dipped her, and kissed her hard and long as he fondled her breast. She could hardly speak as he lifted her upright and walked toward the front door. She shouted after him,

"You can't just leave me like this."

"That's a prelude to tonight's symphony," he teased as he walked out the door.

While Jack was running late, Matt made his usual morning call.

"Hi Daddy, only two more days," Laura cried.

"How did you know it was me, princess?" he asked.

"Daddy, you know *you're* the only one who calls this early in the morning."

"I'm so glad to hear that. You're up extra early for school, aren't you?" he asked.

"I asked Mommy to set my alarm clock so I could talk to you when you called. I called you last night but someone hung up on me," she accused.

"Honey, was that you?" he asked. "My telephone cut off right when I answered it. They still haven't fixed all the cell towers up here," he lied.

"That's okay. I just wanted to remind you that we only had three more days left," she said. "Mommy wants to talk to you. I love you, Daddy, and don't forget, now we have only two more days," she told him.

"I know, and I can't wait either. I have some big hugs and kisses for you," he said as she passed the phone to Katie. "What a way to start my day. She always brings a smile to my face," he told Katie.

"I must admit that she's been great company for me while you've been away. I just want to warn you that she wrote a contract for you to sign agreeing never to go away again," she said.

"Did she really?" he laughed. "Here comes Jack. I'll talk to you tomorrow. I love you, babe," he added before he hung up still chuckling about Laura's contract.

As usual, Julie wondered about who Matt could possibly be talking to every morning, as she watched him from the window. He was always smiling and very animated as he paced back and forth. For the first time she felt a pang of doubt about Matt. Could he be lying to her for the past few weeks, she mused but only for a fleeting moment. She could only imagine that it had to be Kevin or one of the guys from work and she went on with her day.

She was going to treat herself to a new piece of lingerie after Matt promised her a private symphony tonight, and she might offer a movement of her own for him, feeling her body ache for him in anticipation of the night ahead.

Julie was just walking out of Victoria's Secret with her new treasure when she eyed David crossing the street toward her. She made a dash for her car but he was at her side before she could get the key in the door.

"Do you have something there you want to model for me?" he asked.

"It's not for you, David, and I'm running late. I'm sorry, but I really am in a big rush," she said as she got into her car and left him standing on the street. That was a close one, she thought, as she drove away. She couldn't give him the opportunity to upset her and possibly drag that horrible dream about Matt to the surface again. As for David, he stood on the curb looking after her and wondering just how long it would be before that creep would leave.

Julie was waiting at the door for Matt when he got home because they were running late for bowling. She practically pushed him out the door telling him they had to rush. He certainly understood since he didn't want to forfeit the first game for being tardy either.

"We can eat at the lanes. Betty serves great food," Julie told him.

"That's great because I'm starved," he said.

The teams were already warming up and preparing to start their first game as Julie and Matt entered the bowling alley. He ran to find a house ball, hoping it would be the same one he had used for the last two weeks, while Julie ran and ordered their food to be delivered to lane five where Carol and Vinnie were waiting for them. They met back at their lane just in time to start the night. They were bowling against the Anchors tonight. The balls began to roll and the fun began.

"I'm sorry to hear that you were sick last week. I'm glad to see you are back to your old self," said Carol.

"Oh, c'mon, he was just sandbagging," chided Vinnie as he smiled.

"I brought my doctor's note just in case you would say that," Matt bantered back.

"You really weren't looking too good last week," said Vinnie sincerely.

"Are you referring to my bowling?" quipped Matt.

"That's a good one," laughed Vinnie.

"Hey, would you two pay attention? Matt, you're up!" scolded Julie. The Ten Pins took the first two games and started the third. Matt made up for last week by bowling well over his average.

All night, bowlers stopped by their lane to watch Matt's unique curve ball, which hugged the edge of the gutter but swiftly turned in at the very last minute and knocked down all ten pins. Eventually, all the other bowlers were standing behind his lane holding their breath in anticipation of a perfect game as he bowled his last frame. The stress didn't seem to affect him, but everyone else, including his teammates, was white-knuckled with the suspense. He took the bowler's stance, took his steps, and released the ball exactly as he had the prior ones. The pins gave a resounding smack as all ten of them collided and fell. The whole league and spectators clapped and cheered for his perfect game of three hundred. Julie proudly ran up and gave him a big hug and kiss.

"You weren't kidding when you said you would make up for last week," said a shocked Vinnie. "You are staying tonight to celebrate, aren't you?" he added.

"Of course!" Matt agreed.

Julie was happy for Matt and didn't want to spoil his moment, but she was disappointed since she had other plans for them tonight. She trailed behind as Matt was escorted into the bar by his entourage of fans. Two hours later and after countless congratulatory shots, Matt was barely standing as Julie helped him into the car and into bed when they got home. Well, there's always tomorrow night, she thought and wondered how Matt would feel in the morning.

THURSDAY, OCTOBER 27

Julie never expected to see Matt spring out of bed in the morning the way he did, after all the celebrating that he had done the night before.

"Honey, how are you feeling?" she asked.

"Fabulous," he said, as he blew her a kiss and jumped in the shower. Go figure, she thought, as she climbed out of bed exhausted. He had more energy than she did, instead of a severe hangover! Matt was more excited than usual, but he never let on why. Julie assumed it was the thrill of bowling the perfect game last night that had energized him. The thought of his great accomplishment put her in a fantastic mood.

At breakfast, he advised her he would not be coming home from work that evening and that he was going out with the guys.

"It may be a late night, so please don't wait up for me. Remember they're a wild bunch," he said.

"That's great that you're having a night out. I hope you have a good time; the fellas I know in the group can be a lot of fun."

"Julie, I really want to tell you how much I've appreciated all that you have done for me. We've had a great time together, haven't we?" he asked.

"The best," she said. Her heart was beginning to beat faster waiting for him to go further.

"I'm glad I met you. You are a very special person. I really want you to know that," he said.

Julie was sitting on the edge of her chair, still waiting to hear his proposals for their future. "Matt, we really need to talk."

Instead, he looked at the clock and jumped up. "Sure, but now I'm late for Jack!" he said as reached for her; then he hugged and kissed her for what seemed like forever before he ran out the door. He couldn't deal with any more than what he just gave her.

Julie was disappointed; just when she thought they were making progress with their relationship. He had spoken more personally to her this morning than he had in their most intimate moments. She understood that he was extremely shy when it came to sharing his personal thoughts. She was determined to wait up tonight for Matt. She needed to know her own prospects for the future. Could she have been living in a fantasy world?

"Hi Daddy, we only have one more day!" Laura shouted as she answered the phone. "I just can't wait. Mommy said she'll pick me up from school early tomorrow so we can get ready for your party." Matt could hear Katie in the background asking Laura for the phone.

When Katie answered, he said,

"I've never had two women fighting over me before."

Katie answered him, "You would think that she was the wife and I was the maid, the way she's ordering me around with instructions for your party. But it will be worth it once we have you back home with us. I can't wait."

"I can't wait either. I gotta go; Jack is driving down the street. I am so looking forward to seeing you both and giving you big hugs," he said, as he blew kisses and hung up.

"Hi Jack," Matt said as he got into the car. Jack grunted something back and Matt knew he wasn't in his usual good mood. "I bowled a perfect game last night," he told him.

"That's nice," he said.

"Are you going out with the gang tonight?" he asked Jack.

"No, I have something to do. Anyway, I'm not a good drinker when I have something on my mind. I wouldn't want to be sorry later for something I may say," he explained.

"I hope everything straightens itself out for you soon because I really hate to see you in this kind of mood," said Matt, unaware that Jack's remarks were directed toward him.

Lunch at the Sahara was slow, and Julie found herself sitting at the bar talking to Dennis while she watched for customers at the door. He was glad to hear that she hadn't had any more cramping and that she was back to herself.

"So, how are things going?" he asked Julie.

"Great," she answered. "Matt started talking this morning about our future, but then he realized the time and had to run out to meet Jack. At least we're making *some* progress."

Maggie and Marilyn came in for lunch. Julie jumped up and ran to meet them.

"Hello, Julie, how is that dashing prince of yours?" Marilyn asked.

"He's just wonderful," Julie said smiling.

"We're so happy to hear that," Maggie answered. "We were hoping to have the two of you for dinner next week."

"How nice of you both! I'll check with him and let you know. Everything has been going great," she said with a dubious excitement. She seated them at their favorite table and went to get their drinks, which Dennis had already mixed. Marilyn and Maggie were not only frequent diners but also creatures of habit, so the entire staff was familiar with their routine. Luckily for Julie other customers began streaming in for lunch, making the day go faster for her since she probably wouldn't be seeing Matt until tomorrow morning.

Near the end of her shift, Julie received a call from a co-worker, Alexa, asking her if she could possibly work her shift that night. Alexa was really sick and was desperate for a cover since she wouldn't be able to function properly. Julie didn't mind since she wanted to keep busy instead of sitting home alone tonight. Dennis was working a double also and was delighted that Julie was staying for the next shift.

"Yeah, Dennis, I know—'misery loves company'," she said.

"Oh, you know you love working with me," he teased.

"That I do," she said.

The dinner shift was much busier than the lunch shift had been, to Julie's delight. She and Dennis shared snide remarks about some of their annoying customers while they hustled and bustled about. Neither of them was happy with a couple of loud-mouthed braggadocios sitting at the bar discussing their naïve girlfriends, who trusted them and knew nothing about their infidelities. Dennis had to ask them more than once to keep it down, not only because of the offensive content of their conversation but also because of their volume. Dennis and Julie were both glad to see them leave.

Close to the end of her shift, another annoying person walked in.

"Hello, David," she sighed, as he approached her for a kiss on the cheek.

"I was actually lonely tonight and thought I would stop by and see if you were working or if maybe your friend was here so I could finally meet him," he said sincerely. Julie sensed a change in him. He was more humble and mellow than he had been lately. She hoped it was because he had accepted that she loved Matt. She actually felt guilty about her initial reaction to him earlier.

"Matt isn't here, but why don't you take a seat at the bar and wait for me. I'm finishing up a table and I have almost all my shift work done," she told him.

He smiled to see she was receptive to his visit because he truly wanted to be near her tonight. He thought Matt would have been gone by now. Maybe he was wrong and Matt was planning to leave his wife and kid but was putting everything in place before he told Julie. David's hopes would be shattered, but as much as it hurt, he felt a need to keep in contact with Julie. What was worse for him was that he couldn't discuss it anymore with her, unless she brought the subject up.

Dennis had David's drink waiting for him on the bar as he took a seat.

"Hey David," Dennis said.

"Hi," David responded glumly.

"You don't seem too happy," said Dennis.

"Would you expect me to be under these circumstances? She really loves him. And I thought he was only a passing fad," he said. Dennis had known David for years, even before he and Julie had met. He felt badly for him at this moment despite David's past indiscretion. Dennis knew that David truly loved Julie and wanted her back in the worst way.

"You're going to have to let it play out regardless of how long it takes. It hasn't been that long and anything can happen. Even if she moves, you just have to keep in contact with her. If worse comes to worse, you may have to settle on a very dear friendship," Dennis said.

"What do you think of the guy?" David asked Dennis.

"I am starting to have my own suspicions about him, but I can't put my finger on it. Wait a minute! You mean you haven't met him yet?" Dennis responded shocked. "

"No, the opportunity never arose, but I have asked Julie for an introduction. I think she may be afraid that I may do or say something stupid or antagonistic," he said. With that, Julie returned to the bar and took a seat next to David.

"Can you stay and have a drink with me or do you have to rush home?" David asked her.

"Matt is out with his co-workers tonight, so I'll stay for a drink," she agreed. The one drink turned out to be two more drinks as the three of them shared stories from their past and laughed together, just like old times.

It had been a long time since Julie felt as comfortable with David as she did at this moment, but she realized it was because Matt was not being discussed. She would have to leave Matt out of the equation for the time being, as she and David were enjoying this short time together. Julie believed she would probably be moving soon, but that was another subject she would not bring up tonight while David was being so agreeable.

They left the Sahara on good terms and David was happy that Julie was so congenial toward him and even seemed to enjoy his company. He would do anything he could to keep it this way even if it meant accepting Matt.

The fellows took Matt up on his suggestion that they go to Conor's Bar. Some of them had never been there before even though they were from the area. Matt was glad to see some of the regulars there. Allie welcomed the new patrons, especially those who were young and single. They would definitely be a welcome change to her usual conversations and routine. Tommy and Billy were lively as usual. Whether their debates were sports, work, politics, or any other topic, they turned it into a comedy act without even trying.

"What's the occasion?" Allie asked Matt.

"Some of the guys are leaving tomorrow," he said.

"What about you?" she asked.

"It's still up in the air," he lied. As soon as he walked away from the bar to talk to Tommy, who was sitting at one of the tables, she rushed over to Theresa and Karly, who were sitting across the bar. She quickly told them the new scoop.

"Matt must be staying to work something out with Julie since the other guys are leaving tomorrow." The three were delighted for Julie, whom they held in great esteem. Allie had to run to the other side of the bar to cater to her other customers.

FRIDAY, OCTOBER 28

Matt awoke to a dark and dreary morning. He had purposely risen early to pack his belongings without waking Julie, so he could leave without any drama or emotion. He figured she had known it was temporary and had even said so herself. After all, he had said his good-bye yesterday. Matt had packed his duffle bag with only the items he had come with, he took one last look at the peacefully sleeping Julie and left her house for the last time.

Jack was exceptionally quiet this morning when he picked Matt up a half hour earlier as agreed.

"I was hoping you would change your mind about the way you're leaving, that's all," Jack responded when Matt inquired about his silence.

"I can't, so please let's leave it at that. Julie and I talked last night," he fibbed. Then he quickly changed the subject. "So what are the work plans for today?" he asked.

"Not much," Jack answered. "We all have to meet at the union hall, probably for an overall assessment and speeches of gratitude to you and the other out-of-towners. The hall is also putting out a lunch spread for you guys, but I just want to let you know that our team is insisting on taking you out to lunch on our own. I told them I would leave it up to you."

"That would be nice, but they don't have to do that." Jack thought it was strange that Matt could handle a good-bye with the guys that he worked and bonded with for the last month, but not the woman he slept with and who tended to his every comfort. He would make it a point to check on Julie over the next couple of days since he didn't know where she stood with the situation.

The union hall echoed with the rowdy voices of over five hundred electricians and utility workers who were excited at their accomplishment. The nearly four-week male bonding session was coming to an end, but not without mixed feelings on the part of the men. Although the out-of-towners were glad to be going home to their families, some had struck up new friendships and were sad to leave their new buddies. Many exchanged cell numbers and e-mail addresses and agreed to keep in touch.

It didn't take Matt and Jack long to find their group since they assembled at the same spot as on their first day of orientation. Jack was right; the meeting became a ritual of statistics, accolades, and, of course, heartfelt thanks to all the men. The out-of-towners at this point just wanted to eat and start home. Many had hours of travel ahead of them.

After the meeting, Kevin made his way over to Matt in anticipation.

"Listen, Matt, I'd like to get going as soon as possible. The weather doesn't look too great, and I'd like to beat the rain as well as the NYC commuter traffic if I can."

"That's fine with me," Matt said. "I'll just grab something to eat for the ride and say good-bye to the guys and we can start out." He turned to Jack and the crew and explained he wouldn't be able to go out to lunch with them after all. They were very disappointed but understood the desire to avoid NYC traffic at any cost, since all of them at some time had experienced the nightmare. Matt shared a bear hug with each of the group and promised to keep in touch. Jack was sure that would never happen. When it came time to say good-bye to Jack, Matt stood facing him like a guilty school-boy as Jack extended his hand to shake.

"Thanks, Matt, for all your help."

"It was my pleasure," returned Matt, then started, "Look, I want...," but Jack just turned and walked away. He had nothing more to say to Matt. Matt picked up his duffle bag and coat and found Kevin waiting nearby.

"Are you ready?" he asked as they walked out of the union hall.

The skies were ominous, and Matt now understood why Kevin wanted to get a jump on it. It began to drizzle, but the two were hoping to avoid the downpour that was threatening their commute home. Matt's thoughts began to wander as he eagerly imagined the coming home party that awaited him from his two biggest fans.

EPILOGUE

Julie was sitting in her wheelchair looking out the window unaware that David was standing in the doorway watching her. She had come a long way this past eighteen months, he thought, and he was so grateful she had survived her tragedy. He had loved her for so long that he couldn't remember when he started. He did know, though, that he would see her through anything and would love her until the day he died. He couldn't believe she was giving him a second chance. There would never be anyone else for him.

He didn't want to startle her so he cleared his throat and quietly called to her, "Hello there, Julie. So how was your therapy today?" She turned her wheelchair around to face him.

"Great," she answered. "In fact, Keith says that if I keep up the good work, I will be walking down the aisle to meet you at the altar next month. He is such a therapy tyrant; he pushes me to the limit every day, but I appreciate every minute of it. I am so lucky to have him."

"I'm glad to hear that, but I don't care if you wheel or walk down that aisle, as long as you meet me at the altar."

"What brings you here at this time of the day? Shouldn't you be at the office?" she asked. Before he could answer her, the telephone rang. She stopped him from reaching for it by saying, "Stop David! I can get it myself. Remember, I am not an invalid. I am only temporarily incapacitated. Please let me."

She answered on the third ring, and David noticed her face suddenly become pale.

"Yes, I know who this is," she said. "I recognized your voice. And, yes, I am surprised to hear from you after all these months." Now David began to feel faint. He thought, no, it can't be him. Why now? She's come so far; she nearly died because of him. I won't let him do this to her again. As if she were reading his mind, she turned her wheelchair away and continued speaking. "You say you're back in the area and wondering if I want to get together."

David wanted to grab the phone from her and hang it up but he knew better. He would have to stand by and let her take care of this. She had been hoping for this opportunity but never thought it would happen for she never thought she would ever hear from Matt again. David hoped it wouldn't set her back emotionally, yet he understood how badly she needed closure in order to move on. Next month they were going to be married, and he wanted them to live happily ever after.

He stood nearby and watched as she struggled to compose herself while she answered the caller softly and calmly,

"You ask how I've been. Well, let's see, after six months in the hospital, three of them in intensive care with nearly every bone in my body broken, six months in a rehab learning to live again, and the last six at home confined to a wheel chair with extensive daily therapy, I guess you might say I am happy to be alive. I'm sorry; did you ask what happened to me?"

David was amazed at how in control she remained.

"Remember the last day you were here, that morning you left the house without so much as a good-bye? The day you conveniently forgot to tell me that your temp work here was over and that you were going home that evening to your real home in New Jersey? That you were going home to your wife and child that you denied ever having? Well, when you didn't come home that night, I began to panic. It was such a bleak rainy night with dense blinding fog that I feared something had happened to you when you didn't come home and that you were left stranded and hurt somewhere. I began calling everywhere—the police, the local bars, the fire department, the hospitals—, but no one knew or had heard anything. I even called some of the guys you worked with up here. They just said that you'd gone home, which I understood to mean my house.

"My panic turned into despair as I raced out of the house without my coat or cell phone. I began to drive not knowing where to look first. I decided to start at the Sahara thinking you and some of the guys stopped off for a drink. When I didn't find you there, I thought maybe you decided on Conor's instead. But when no one there had set eyes on you, my fear became terror. By that time, the rain was falling in torrents, and I couldn't see an inch in front of me. As I pulled away, I hit a puddle, my car hydroplaned, and I skidded off the road into a ravine. They told me months later that my car had turned over a couple of times before it came to a stop and burst into flames. I thank God for the fast-thinking witnesses who pulled me out of the car and called for help.

"Now, aren't you glad you called? I am. I've had a reversal of fortune and feel as though my life has turned around completely since then and I consider myself the luckiest woman on this earth. Unfortunately, I can't say the same for your wife. What kind of creature are you anyway? You disguised your identity and tried to pass yourself off as someone else; you just fit in perfectly, didn't you? You say you're sorry. I lost a baby in that accident and will never be able to have another. *That* is sorry," she said. For the first time since she picked up the phone, Julie turned toward David and continued, "It was so nice of you to call me after all this time, but don't call me again. I am marrying the most wonderful man in the world- a *real* gentleman!"

She hung up the telephone and sat shaking uncontrollably as David embraced her with all his might. After some time passed, she managed to calm down, and David poured her a snifter of brandy, insisting she drink it. She sat very still for a moment, then looked him intently in the eyes and said softly,

"N*ow* I can marry you in peace."

ABOUT THE AUTHOR

P. A. Schweizer currently resides in New Jersey and is retired from a major communications corporation after thirty years. She held a second job as a waitress for twenty-eight of those years. Her son is a successful spinal surgeon and raising him is what she considers to be her greatest accomplishment. Schweizer loves travelling, reading, and Broadway shows. Her second novel, *The Gentleman's Demise*, will both stun and surprise her many fans!

Schweizer's website: schweizerread.info

Made in the USA
Middletown, DE
17 April 2024